D1295612

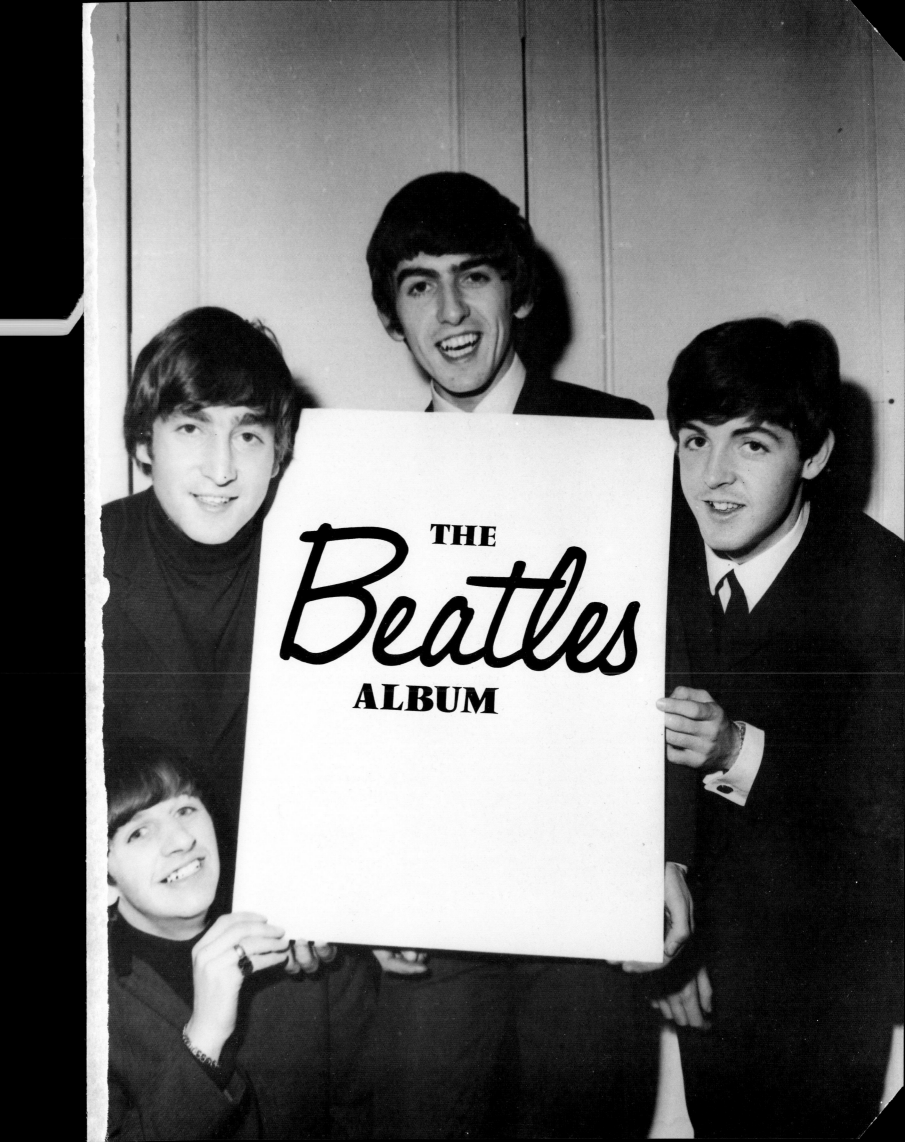

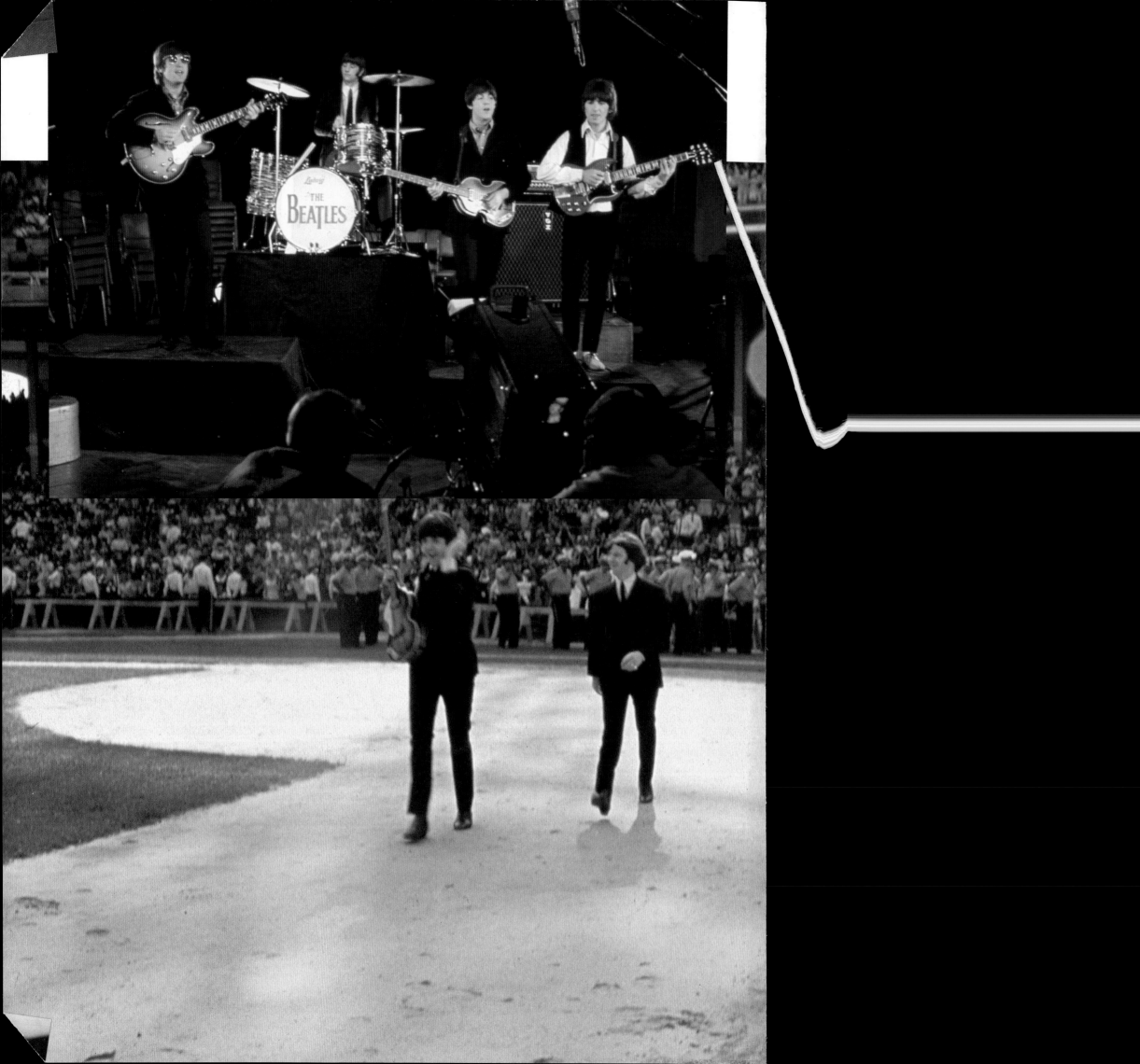

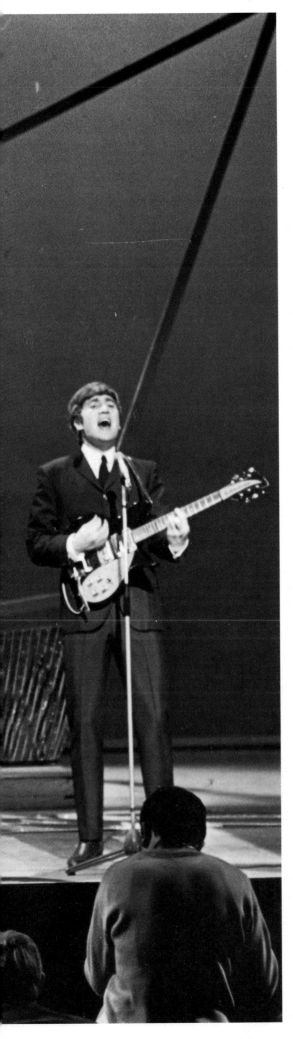

CONTENTS

Page 1 The Beatles in the heady days of 1968 with their two-record set with a totally white jacket, forever known simply as 'The White Album'.

Pages 2 and 3 The Beatles play the huge Shea Stadium, New York, on their 1965 trip to the US.

Left On stage at the London Palladium in October 1963; Beatlemania is just beginning.

INTRODUCTION

The Beatles were, are, and will no doubt continue to be an unmatched and unmatchable musical phenomenon, in John Lennon's words the 'Greatest Show on Earth'. They were the biggest concert draw, the largest earners, the topselling band of the 1960s – and 20 years after they stopped recording, their recordings still outsell many current groups. And yet they were four ordinary lads from Liverpool, as they continued to delight in proving through the famous years, by demanding chip butties in elegant hotels, ignoring pomposity and protocol, and never losing their characteristically Scouse sense of humor.

Certainly the early years were neither particularly easy nor particularly out of the ordinary. John, raised by his redoubtable Aunt Mimi after his parents' marriage disintegrated, funny and angry in turns; Paul, a quiet clever one, brought up by a devoted father after his mother's early death; George, youngest of a large and loving family; Ringo, only child of a marriage that ended three years after his birth, in hospital for a year at age six and two years in his teens.

And yet between them they put their finger on the musical pulse of a generation and kept it there for nearly ten years. From the first hit, 'Love Me Do' in 1963, to 'Abbey Road', the last album , they caught and led the musical taste of their contemporaries worldwide. The early thumping irresistible rock numbers gave way in 1965 to something more complex, both lyrically and musically, with the single 'Yesterday' and the album 'Rubber Soul'. 'Revolver' the following year also broke new ground, with its continuous almost narrative performance. The Sergeant Pepper album became the ultimate symbol of the counter-culture that bloomed in the 1967 Summer of Love, while the 'White Album' in 1968 was not only a tour de force of musical and lyrical creativity but also a synthesis of all the Beatles had learned about studio technique. In the 1960s pop music moved from infancy to maturity with the Beatles in the lead.

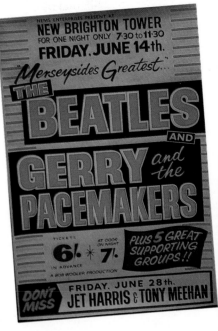

Left A self-conscious pose for Stuart Sutcliffe, flanked by George Harrison (left) and John Lennon (right) on the first tour to Hamburg in 1960. Stu learned to play bass guitar in order to join the Silver Beatles.
Above This poster dates from 1963, when it was all beginning to come together for the Beatles.

Above By 1964 they were breaking records regularly – in February they made their first visit to the US and drew an estimated television audience of 50 million for their second performance in a week on the Ed Sullivan Show.

Left The Beatles in 1966.

Left and below left On stage at the London Palladium, 1964, and the realities of the touring life.

Below right John and Paul in 1968, soon after their return from India and the release of 'Lady Madonna'.

Right above The Beatles together on the set of *The Magic Christian* in 1969, in which Ringo starred with Peter Sellers.

Right below The Beatles launching the 'Sergeant Pepper' album at the Apple headquarters in London, June 1967.

Above John, Ringo and Paul show off the MBEs they were awarded in June 1965.

Left, far left and below Help!, the Beatles' second film, was as fantastic as *A Hard Day's Night*, with the added bonus of exotic locations.

Left The Beatles in 1969, still clowning although they are now living very separate lives.

Below With the Maharishi in India on their joint trip to his ashram in 1968.

Bottom left Paul after founding his own group, Wings.

Bottom right The touring days – London airport in 1965.

BEGINNINGS

TO END OF 1963

John Winston Lennon was the first of the future Beatles to form a group, the Quarrymen, in 1956 while he was still a reluctant pupil at Liverpool's Quarry Bank High School. He invited the left-handed guitarist Paul McCartney, who attended the prestigious Liverpool Institute, to join them soon after, and George Harrison, also at the Institute but a couple of years junior, drifted in in 1958. As the British skiffle craze gave way to American-inspired rock, the Quarrymen became Johnny and the Moondogs and included Stuart Sutcliffe, whom John met at art college.

The name Silver Beatles was adopted on the spur of the moment in April 1960 for an audition with pop promoter Larry Parnes, who gave them their first formal booking. In August through Allan Williams, owner of the Jacaranda coffee bar and a budding entrepreneur, they found themselves playing the Kaiserkellar in rough and seedy Hamburg, with Pete Best on drums. Another Liverpool group, Rory Storm and the Hurricanes, was also there, with their drummer Richard Starkey. In Hamburg they met artist and photographer Astrid Kirschner, who cut their hair and persuaded first

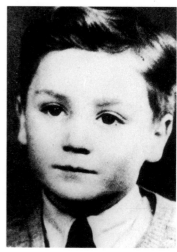

Left A soulful Lennon in his primary school uniform.

Far left 9 Newcastle Road, Liverpool, where John spent his first five years with his mother Julia Stanley.

Below Dovedale Primary, John's first school.

Right above George, John and Paul in moody pose in Hamburg, 1960, with Teddy Boy rig-out and sleeked-back Tony Curtis hairstyle.

Right below Picture taken by John in Arnhem cemetery. Allan Williams, then manager of the Beatles, is on the far left; Stuart Sutcliffe wears dark glasses; Paul, George and Pete Best are seated left to right.

Stuart and then the others out of their battered jeans and into well cut black leather. In Hamburg too they learned to survive on pep pills, beer, cigarettes and precious little sleep – and Lennon and McCartney got together as a team and began to write their own material.

By May 1961, after a second trip to Hamburg when Stu decided to stay with Astrid, the Beatles found themselves famous on the Liverpool scene, and were signed by hopeful young music store manager Brian Epstein. He persuaded George Martin of EMI to audition the Beatles, now back to four, and they were signed to the Parlophone label in July 1962. It was clear to Martin that Pete Best was musically the weak link, and Brian reluctantly replaced him with Richard Starkey, by now universally known by his stage name of Ringo Starr. After initial doubts, Martin agreed that the Beatles' first release should be a Lennon-McCartney number, 'Love Me Do', which made it to a respectable number 17 in the record charts. The next release was 'Please Please Me' – by then Brian had found a hungry music publisher, Dick James, keen to promote what he regarded as an exciting new sound. He got the Beatles a spot on the influential pop show *Thank Your Lucky Stars*, 'Please Please Me' topped the charts – and Beatlemania was on its way.

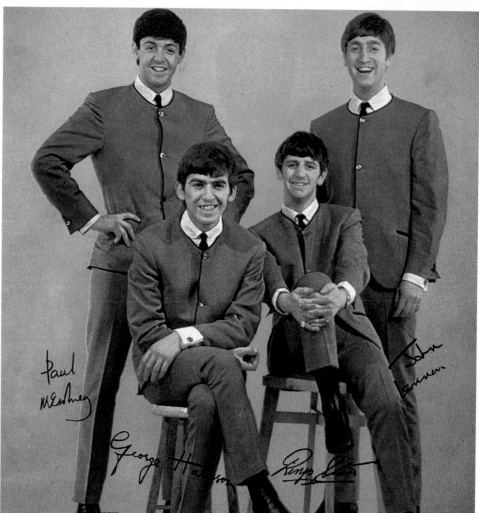

Above The Cavern Club in Liverpool, where the Beatles became resident group in 1961.

Left and below Beatles souvenirs had become big business by 1963.

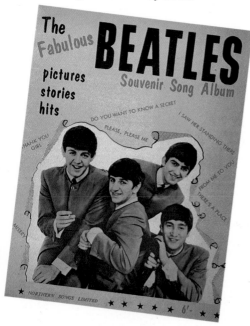

Right A carefully posed studio shot from 1963.

Above Pete Best in 1964, two years
after he was sacked from the Beatles.

Right above Pete on drums with
George, Paul, John and Davy Jones at
The Cavern in 1961.

Right below The Beatles in their
leather look, 1961.

17

Left 10 Admiral Grove, where Ringo lived from the age of 11 with his mother and his stepfather Harry Graves.

Above George was born at 12 Arnold Grove, Wavertree, and lived there with his parents, sister Louise and brothers Harold and Peter until he was six.

Right Jacaranda, 23 Slater Street, the seedy coffee bar where John and Stu Sutcliffe used to spend their time. The owner was Allan Williams, who first featured their group as Johnny and the Moondogs and went on to become manager of the Silver Beatles.

Left Ringo (second from left) with Rory Storm and the Hurricanes at Butlins, Skegness, in 1961. They were Liverpool's biggest group; it was at Butlins that Richard Starkey finally became Ringo Starr.

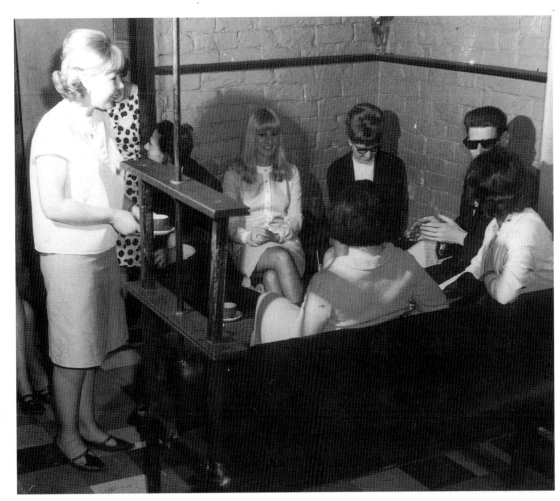

Below Paul passed his 11-plus exam in 1952 and went to the Liverpool Institute. He did well there and was always in the top streams; he had the knack of doing just enough work to get by.

Above The Beatles on a
Liverpool bomb site in
1962, soon after they were
signed by George Martin at
Parlophone and replaced
Pete Best with Ringo.

Right The Blue Angel Club
in Liverpool, where John,
Paul, George and Stu
Sutcliffe auditioned before
Larry Parnes, king of rock
and roll, in 1960. Parnes
wanted a backing group for
Billy Fury; he offered the
Silver Beatles, a name they
invented on the spur of the
moment, their first proper
engagement, a two-week
tour of Scotland.

Right above Paul in relaxed
mood with friends,
including Len Garry, ex-
member of the Quarrymen.

Right below The Beatles
performing in The Cavern,
where it all began, in 1962.

POST
BUNDES 20 DEUTSCHE
POST
BUNDES 15 DEUTSCHE

HAMBURG 1
11.11.62-12

Mrs. Violent Stubb
54. Broadgreen Road.
Liverpool
ENGLAND.

— Made in Western Germany —

Darling Vi,

We are all missing you so much, you will never know. To caress your feet once more would be just heaven, also to hold your lungs in mine and drink T.B. John sends you all his lunch also Paul and Ringworm greet too! As I write this card we are being surrounded by large, black negroes happy at heart and brown of complexion. Its not much very now fun here but only 1 week to go now so its not so bad now. Have the kettle on on Sunday 18th Cheerio love from Geage & and friends xxxxx

Left George in The Cavern in 1961, sporting the leather gear that the Beatles favored at the time. He joined the Quarrymen early in 1958. The postcard home dates from the group's third Hamburg trip, when they had become the Beatles.

22

Above The Beatles in London in 1962. They have been signed by Parlophone and have acquired Ringo, and the early Beatles look is beginning to emerge under the influence of Brian Epstein, who cut their hair and put them into suits. Their first hit is on the way.

Brian Epstein had spent four years building up the family firm of NEMS (North End Music Stores) when he was first asked for a Beatles record in October 1961. By December he was their manager and was already beginning to smarten up their appearance, their presentation and their organization. These shots were taken in Austen Reed, the elegant men's outfitters in London's Regent Street, around the time that 'Please Please Me' was released.

WE ARE NOW ACCEPTING ORDERS FOR

THE BEATLES

FIRST RECORD ON PARLOPHONE

LOVE ME DO

c/w

P.S. I LOVE YOU

RELEASED FRIDAY OCTOBER 5th

N E M S 12-14, WHITECHAPEL. Tel. ROYal. 7895
50, GREAT CHARLOTTE ST. 70-72, WALTON RD.

The new-look Beatles hit the big time in early 1963, with two chart-toppers within three months, 'Please Please Me' and 'Love Me Do'.

In February 1963 the Beatles made their first nationwide tour, although Helen Shapiro was billed as the top attraction. From then on it was all go. In August, when they played at Abbotsfield Park, Manchester, and the Grafton Rooms, Liverpool, they also made their last appearance at The Cavern.

'FAB' FOB BROOCH!

containing 12 photographs of

THE BEATLES

only 4/6 (Inc. Post)

Be with it! order now!

POST THIS COUPON TODAY WITH A POSTAL ORDER TO GIROSIGN LTD., DEPT, "A" 86-88 WARDOUR ST. LONDON W.I.

NAME (block letters) ....

Address (block letters) ....

No personal callers.

GRAFTON ROOMS—This Friday

CHICK GRAHAM & The Coasters
SONNY WEBB & The Cascades

THE BEATLES
THE UNDERTAKERS
THE DENNISONS

7-30—8-30
8-30—9-30
9-30—10-00
AND
11-00—11-30
10-00—11-00
11-30—12-30

ADVANCE TICKETS 7/6 USUAL AGENCIES
(The above timings are provisional)

Abbotsfield Park, Urmston, Manchester
AUGUST 5th at 7-30
KENNEDY STREET ENTERPRISES LTD.
Present the Biggest Pop Carnival ever to be held in a marquee!
A TWIST & SHOUT DANCE
Starring
THE BEATLES
Brian Poole & the Tremeloes
The Dennisons
Johnny Martin & The Tremors
Tickets from Nems, Liverpool or Lewis's, Manchester, or Three Coins, Manchester: Admission 10/6 plus 2/6 entrance fee to The Urmston Show : : The Urmston Show commences at 11-30 a.m.
MAKE THIS A DAY OUT!

George Martin of EMI made a niche for himself in Parlophone, one of EMI's smaller companies, in the 1950s by producing comedy records. As the teenage music scene took off in the early 60s, Parlophone became desperate for a star. Martin originally saw the Beatles as a possible backing group for Cliff Richard. When the Beatles won a silver disc for 'Please Please Me' (*above*), Martin's reputation was made.

Above left and right In August 1963, to coincide with the release of 'She Loves You', the Beatles were in Birmingham making a television show. The usual pre-performance clowning was caught in a photo session, with Paul and a turbaned John displaying their musical skills.

Above On the night of October 13 1963 at the London Palladium, the Beatles were transformed from just another pop group into a journalist's dream. An estimated audience of 15,000,000 watched the show live on television, and the theater was besieged by screaming fans all day – Beatlemania was beginning.

Left Success brings the finer things of life for the Liverpool lads – candles, wine, linen and silverware.

The Royal Variety Performance on November 4 1963 was the Beatles' second big London date, and a much more select affair than the Palladium. Tickets were four times the usual price and it was a charity show, attended by the Queen Mother, Princess Margaret and her husband Lord Snowdon. The atmosphere was usually distinctly sycophantic, with the audience waiting to see how each act was received by the Royal Box before clapping. Needless to say the Beatles were unabashed and did their usual act, clowning and joking on stage and causing mayhem in the audience simply by announcing that they were going to sing 'She Loves You'.

Left above With Marlene Dietrich before the show.

Left below The Fab Four, relaxed and confident, rehearsing on the afternoon of the show.

Right above Jumping for joy, a classic Beatles shot.

Right below After a strenuous day rehearsing, the boys relax before their big moment.

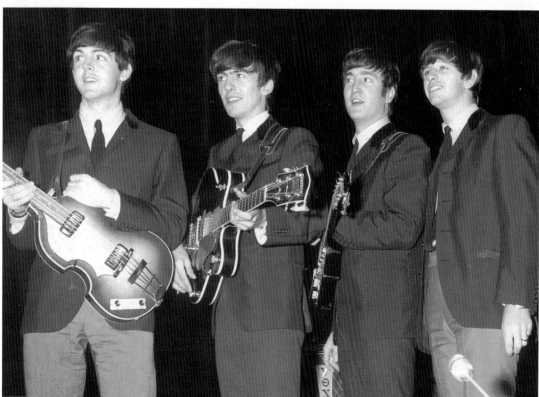

By late 1963 the Beatles were regularly featured on television and even the quality newspapers had got in on the act. On November 1 they began another tour, this time billed simply as the Beatles Show. Here the camera focuses on Paul and Ringo.

Left Packing them in in a Birkenhead cinema, with John and Paul doing their 'Yeah Yeah Yeah' bit.

Above Manufacturers all over the country are leaping on the bandwagon. The collarless Beatle jacket first went on sale in September 1963, and Beatle wigs soon followed.

Right above and below
Another posh venue for the boys, a dinner-jacketed pre-Christmas gathering at the Grosvenor House Hotel in London's Park Lane.

Left Earlier in the autumn the Beatles had toured Sweden, the first foreign trip since Hamburg. Their reception was wild – the normally self-possessed Swedish teenagers stormed the stage at a concert in Stockholm, breaking through a 40-strong police guard and knocking George off his feet.

Left On their return from Sweden on October 29 the Beatles first became aware of their staggering popularity. Thousands of screaming fans besieged London Airport for hours, holding up a car containing the British Prime Minister Sir Alec Douglas-Home, and totally ignoring Miss World.

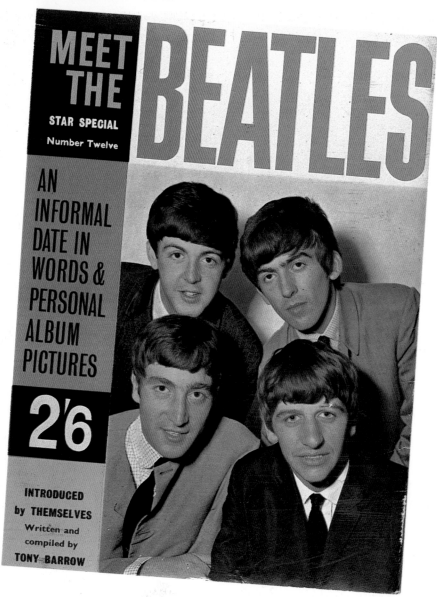

Above left and right The Beatles' departure for their Swedish tour was an altogether calmer and more restrained affair than their return, and George has time to take a picture of the fans.

Left Just one of innumerable 'fanzines' that catered to the insatiable desire for information about every aspect of the boys' lives. Privacy has become a dream.

Right Another night, another show. Touring, posing for publicity shots, and avoiding the fans becomes a way of life.

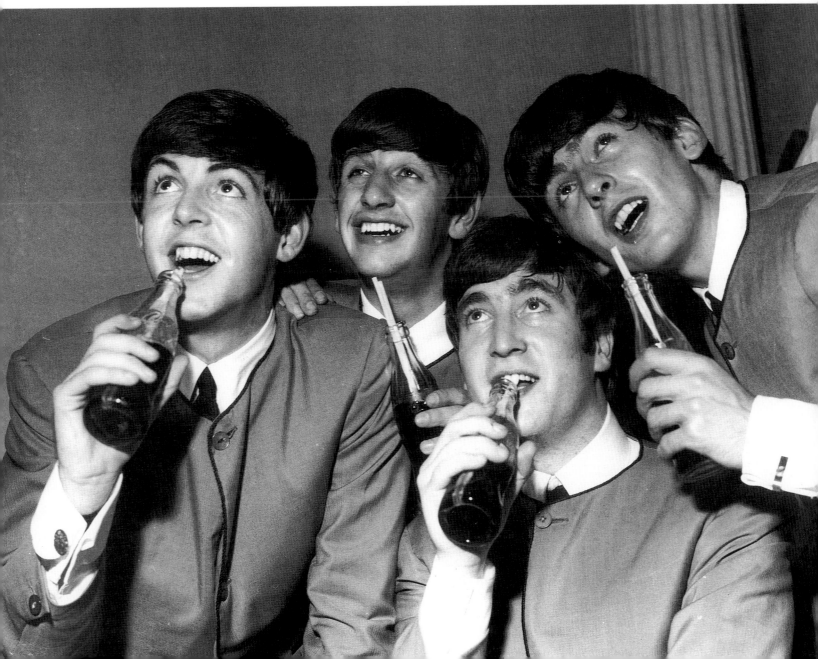

Left Anyone out there want us? Peering round a door at the eagerly awaiting world.

Right From the outset each Beatle had his individual style. Clockwise from top left: a soulful Paul adopts his choirboy look; Ringo strikes a tougher note despite the suit and tie; George, always the silent one, seems to distance himself from the whole proceedings; and John, shortly before publication of his first volume of poetry *In His Own Write*, plays the intellectual.

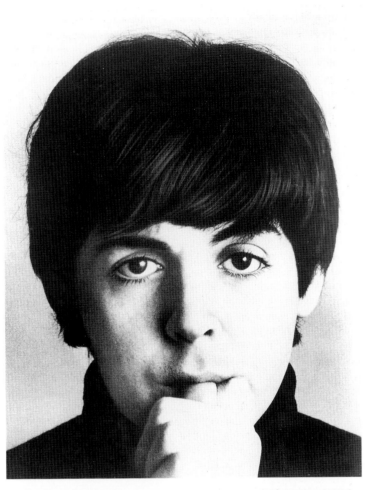
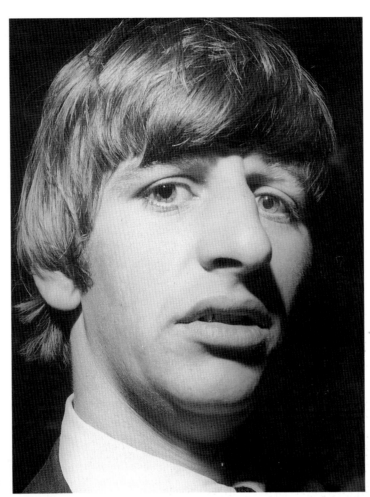

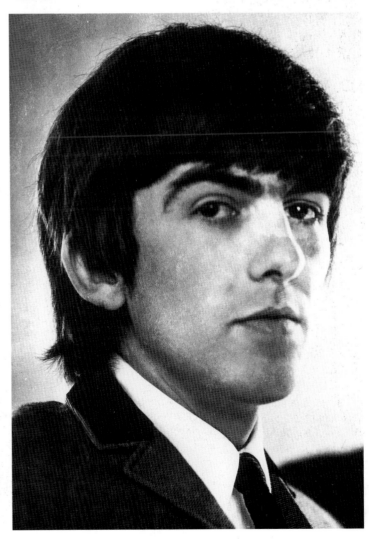

41

Pantomime time for the Beatles at the Astoria, Finsbury Park, one of London's largest theaters. The show was organized by NEMS, Brian Epstein's family company. One of the sketches was a Victorian melodrama – George played the heroine, tied to a railway line by the villainous Sir Jasper (a swashbuckling John in cloak and hat) and rescued by Fearless Paul the Signalman.

Right The Beatles enjoy some of the other turns at the NEMS Christmas show – actually on New Year's Eve, 1963.

Below After the show – Ringo in a happy daze, Paul still raving, as 1963 becomes 1964, the year the Beatles hit America and Beatlemania goes international.

Right The Beatles take over *Juke Box Jury*, a somewhat staid panel game in which a team of four gave scores of one to five to the latest releases. The BBC commandeered the Empire Theater, Liverpool, for this special edition and disgruntled technicians, forced to travel from London, renamed it the Beatles Broadcasting Corporation.

44

Photocall at the Lewisham Theater in
seedy south London, where signs of
bomb damage can still be seen and
the police can hardly hold back the
adoring fans.

BEATLEMANIA

1964-66

The Beatles had begun 1963 as a modestly successful pop group; by early 1964 they were show business legends. In January the Top Twenty was awash with Beatles records. As well as 'I Want to Hold Your Hand' at the top of the charts, six tracks from the 'With the Beatles' album also figured, and the album itself qualified for the singles chart by selling almost a million copies. The effect on the somewhat torpid and conventional music industry was galvanizing. Pop music became both culturally

and socially acceptable; serious articles appeared in the quality newspapers and *The Times* pronounced John and Paul to be 'outstanding composers'.

The next two years were a wild gallop of recording sessions, hotels, concerts, hotels, film-making, touring – and more hotels. The first big challenge was the conquest of the USA. Capitol Records had bought rights to 'I Want to Hold Your Hand' but the media remained cool until the last moment. Americans were still reeling from the assassination of President Kennedy on November 22nd, 1963. In January 1964, however, 'I Want to Hold Your Hand' soared to the top of the US charts and the American press finally discovered the Beatles. Their US tour in February, boldly set up by Brian months before, was guarranteed success; Brian

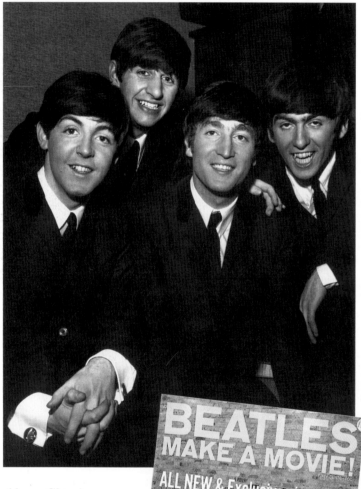

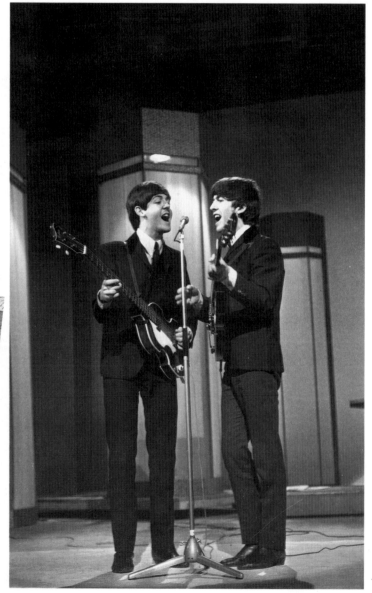

Above Glowing with success as 'I Want to Hold Your Hand' tears into the charts.

Right A Hard Day's Night, the Beatles' first film, was frontline news long before its release.

Far right Paul and George sing 'I Want to Hold Your Hand'.

Above By early 1964 the
Beatles were in constant
demand for live and
television shows; they
were the first group to pack
out Wembley Stadium in
north London with adoring
fans.

Left Arriving in New York
for their first-ever US tour, a
mere two weeks, but they
starred on the coast-to-
coast Ed Sullivan Show.

A classic series of shots of the Beatles in action at the London Palladium, January 1964. As ever they livened things up with a few gags before swinging in to the showbiz routine.

was as staggered as the boys themselves by the scale and fervor of their reception. But this short tour, with a spot on the famous Ed Sullivan Show, was also the Beatles' first real exposure to the limitations such amazing popularity placed on their personal freedom. For the next two years, until they formally gave up touring, they were virtual prisoners.

Filming proved a lively and stimulating outlet for energies that might otherwise have become self-destructive. *A Hard Day's Night* caught exactly the zany and self-deprecating humor that was one of the most endearing qualities of all four Beatles, and one that helped them survive their punishing schedule. And, of course, they spent – cars, houses, country estates, nothing seemed to make a dent in their vast earnings.

Merchandising also took off, Beatles souvenirs became worldwide earners, and in 1965 Northern Songs Ltd, Managing Director Dick James, was launched to market the songs that Lennon and McCartney continued to produce in amazing bursts of creativity.

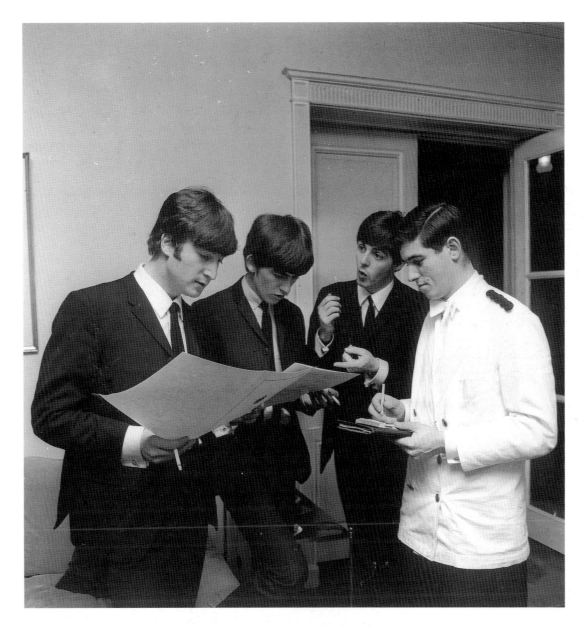

Above and left The Beatles in Paris.
Brian Epstein arranged their second
continental visit as a warming-up
routine for their first US tour. They
spent three weeks in France from
January 15, 1964, playing at the
Olympia in Paris. The first concert
was not a success and the reviews
were lukewarm at the best; *France-
Soir* called them *zazous* (delinquents)
and *vedettes demodées* (has-beens).

Left It was in their suite in the George
V Hotel that the Beatles and Brian
heard that 'I Want to Hold Your Hand'
had topped the American charts –
French insularity ceased to matter.

Above Ordering a meal at the George
V was a serious business.

Above and left The Beatles were given the usual ecstatic send-off from London Airport for their US tour in February. As they flew out on Pan Am flight 101, station WMCA in New York made the first of a series of announcements: 'It is now 6.30 a.m. Beatle time . . . the temperature is 32 Beatle degrees'.

Right above and below After the wild success of the Ed Sullivan Show, the Beatles flew down to Miami to do another; even the pilot wore a Beatle wig.

Above A Beatle chorus in the rolling Atlantic surf.

Below Cruising in the inevitable convertible.

Above Posing with Ed Sullivan after appearing in the show. 50,000 applied for the 728 tickets and the show had a record television audience of 73 million.

Right above A casual shot back in England.

Right below The adoring fans in their prim early sixties gear.

Right and opposite The return from their US tour was even more rapturous than their departure. The welcoming fans took over London Airport altogether. The date was February 25th, George's twenty-first birthday.

Paul (*above left*), Ringo (*above*) and George (*left*) each had his own following – every Beatle fan had his or her favorite. John was the only married one. Cynthia Powell had been in the same year as John at Art College and they met properly at Christmas 1958 in their second year, although it was a long time before quiet middle-class Cynthia dared to introduce John to her parents. They married in 1962 and their son Julian was born in 1963, but Cynthia kept a very low profile; the first US trip was the only time that she accompanied John on tour.

In summer 64 the tours began again
and the Beatles were constantly on
the go. After three months of UK
travel and shows they went first to
continental Europe, beginning in
Denmark, then on to Hong Kong,
Australia and New Zealand, ending
with over a month in the USA in
September.

Left and above Where to now? From
Waterloo Station, London, to
anywhere in the world.

In March the Beatles started shooting their first film *A Hard Day's Night*. The title was only decided at the last moment although John had used it earlier in a poem. The director Richard Lester had cut his teeth on the classic *The Running, Jumping, Standing Still Film* made with the anarchical British comedy team of the Goons.

Left above and below Much of the film was simply intended to show the Beatles being themselves and was shot in television studios, on London streets and in a specially hired train. Here Lester directs a studio sequence.

Right Between takes on the set of *A Hard Day's Night*.

Above Tidying up the famous Beatle hairstyles before filming starts at Twickenham studios. The four hairdressers all had small parts in the film, but Patti Boyd (far left) was to play a rather larger role in George's life. When she met George on the first day of filming she was working as a model and had done a very successful television commercial for Smith's Crisps, directed by Richard Lester, who then offered her a part in the Beatles film.

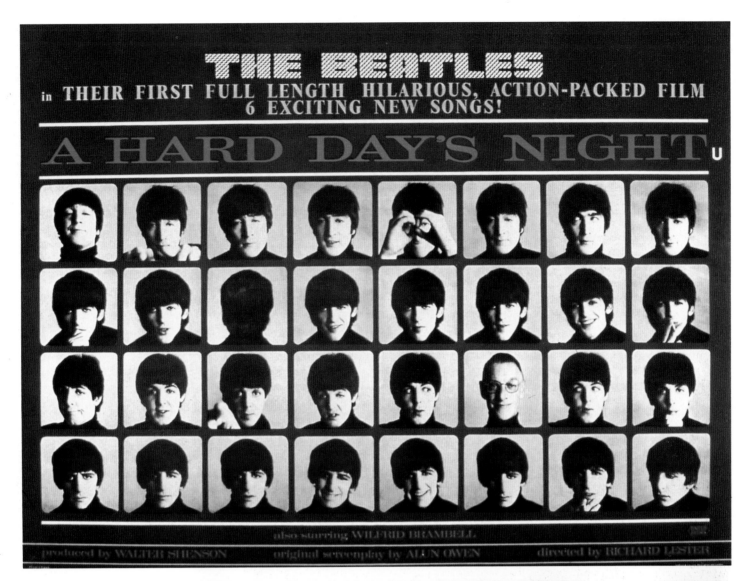

THE BEATLES

in THEIR FIRST FULL LENGTH HILARIOUS, ACTION-PACKED FILM
6 EXCITING NEW SONGS!

A HARD DAY'S NIGHT U

also starring WILFRID BRAMBELL

produced by WALTER SHENSON   original screenplay by ALUN OWEN   directed by RICHARD LESTER

Left Filming *A Hard Day's Night* at Twickenham studios, south-west London; the whole film was shot in six weeks in March and April 1964, between the return from America and the start of summer touring.

Above Publicity poster for the launch of *Hard Day's Night*.

Right A quiet moment for Paul during filming at the Scala Theater London. He was known as the organized hardworking one but here he relaxes with *Today*, a popular weekly.

Left Dick Lester was known for his technical virtuosity, using several cameras to shoot action simultaneously from different angles and relying on ingenious cutting techniques. These shots became a *leitmotif* running through *A Hard Day's Night*.

Above An action shot in a London street – the crew could only film for a few minutes before the stars were recognized and mobbed.

Right Alun Owen's script for *A Hard Day's Night* successfully caught the zany private humor that helped to give the Fab Four their air of self-sufficiency.

Above They may look as
though they're in action but
this is just a pose for the
ever-attendant camera.

Left below Wilfrid Brambell and Norman Rossington, two stalwarts of the British screen, co-starred with the Beatles in *A Hard Day's Night*.

Right Paul and Wilfrid Brambell filming at Marylebone Station, London. Brambell plays Paul's tiresome grandfather, who harasses the boys through a train journey to London and a TV show.

Below A close-up of, from left, Ringo, George, Paul and John, looking tanned and relaxed after their Far East tour in the summer of 1964.

Left Escaping the doting attentions of the fans was a constant problem while shooting *A Hard Day's Night*. After making a train sequence, John is first across the platform, dodging through a taxi and into the waiting chauffeur-driven car, followed by an athletic George and a rather less elegant Ringo.

Above An unusual hairdo for John; the magazine is suitable hair salon reading.

Right George leaps again, this time dramatically silhouetted against the sky, in a shot from the movie.

Above Ringo always seems the odd one out, isolated in the background on his drums.

Right Paul goes solo. Among the other three he was often referred to as 'the star'. When an American reporter asked John when they started rehearsing for the Ed Sullivan Show, he replied: 'We don't, Paul does'.

Above The concert which forms the heart of *A Hard Day's Night* was shot at the Scala Theater, London. The film is a comic fantasia which harnesses all the Beatles's musical and comedy skills, and was an enormous commercial success. Full of cinematic jokes, it had a host of imitators among the swinging London spy thrillers and comedies of the later sixties, but at the time seemed a breath of fresh air.

Left A Lennon leap; John is beginning to get a little chubby with all the high living of success.

Above George and John backstage at the Scala Theater, wearing the neat velvet-collared suits of *A Hard Day's Night*.

Left An unusual rear view showing the enraptured audience as the boys perform and the cameras roll.

75

Far left, above left and right Another
month, another show; filming in
London.

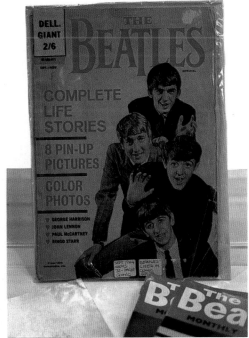

Above and right Fanzines
and souvenirs have really
taken off; the nylon
stockings are Dutch, the
handkerchief American.

Left above What is she doing to John? He seems to be enjoying it in this shot from *A Hard Day's Night*.

Left below A Hard Day's Night has everything – music, comedy, the famous four, and the Folies Bergères.

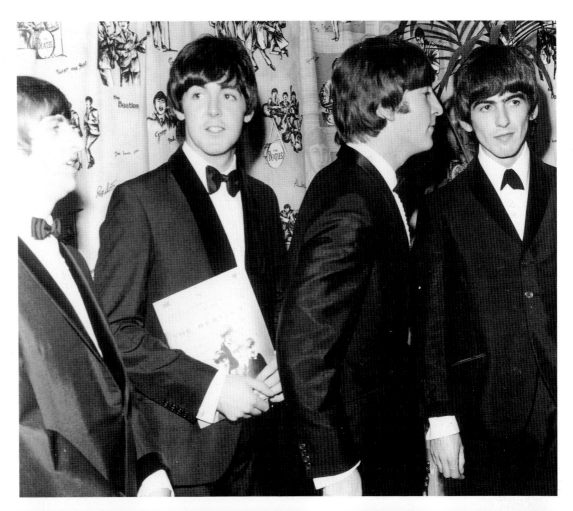

Right The Beatles in more sober mode, but note the curtain fabric.

Left A serious George with model Patti Boyd, who had a small part in the film as a teenage fan.

Above Ringo reads *Anatomy of a Murder* on the set – or is he just daydreaming?

Above In May 1964 the Beatles made
their first solo television show
Around the Beatles, another huge
success. Here Paul and George join
forces.

Above The boys wear the classic collarless Beatles jacket which they made so famous in this still from *A Hard Day's Night*.

Left In the early heady days of success the four always seemed to find time for a bit of clowning. Is it a chip butty they are passing from hand to hand, discreetly wrapped in a handkerchief?

Above John's first book of poetry, *In His Own Write*, was published in March and went straight to the top of the bestseller list. The leading British literary weekly, *The Times Literary Supplement*, said: 'It is worth the attention of anyone who fears for the impoverishment of the English language and the British imagination'. Here John and Cynthia arrive at the Dorchester Hotel, London, where John is to be guest of honor at the annual Foyle's Literary Lunch.

Left Paul and Ringo spar with boxer Henry Cooper, who seems to be warning Ringo to pick on someone his own size.

Above The Foyle's lunch was and is a glitzy occasion, much cherished by London literati and showbiz personalities. John is seated next to impresario Lionel Bart, composer of the hit musical *Oliver!*, while behind him stand violinist Yehudi Menuhin and author, cartoonist and classic English eccentric Osbert Lancaster.

Left A solemn John in his crumpled corduroy is caught in the foyer of the Dorchester.

Left and above In May the Beatles made their *Around the Beatles* television show, which included the scene from Shakespeare's *A Midsummer Night's Dream* where the 'rude mechanicals' act out the sad history of Pyramus and Thisbe for the nobles of the Athenian court. *Left* The lovers, movingly played by Paul and John, are divided by a wall. George plays the moon (*above right*), witness to the unfolding of the tragedy, and Ringo (*above left*) is the savage lion who consumes the unfortunate Thisbe before she can be united with her lover – while reassuring the audience that he is not really a fierce lion and promising to roar gently so as not to alarm them.

Above When the Beatles began their summer's touring in June, Ringo was unable to accompany them – he had collapsed the day before with laryngitis and tonsillitis. The last-minute substitute seen with (*from left*) Paul, John and George on the steps of the plane for Copenhagen is Jimmy Nicol, drummer with the Blue Flames, Georgie Fame's backing group.

Left The Fab Four continued to cultivate the more formal look that Brian Epstein gave them through the hard touring days of 1964 and 1965.

Left The classic mop-haired look that was the Beatles' trademark. In this still from *A Hard Day's Night* they seem to be planning a quick get-away.

Below A more casual look for the boys as they tour Cliveden, elegant Thames-side home of the well-known Astor family.

Left After his recovery from laryngitis, Ringo flew out to join the other three Beatles in Adelaide, Australia, in June 1964. This shot shows him at London Airport with Brian Epstein, who usually managed to stay very much in the background on Beatle tours but organized their itinerary to the last detail.

Above Film star Vivien Leigh, who made her name in *Gone With the Wind* and subsequently married British actor Laurence Olivier, was on the same flight as Ringo.

Right Ringo enjoying the undivided attention of the media at London Airport before leaving for Australia.

After Hong Kong the Beatles moved on to a rapturous reception in Australia. In the foyer of the Sheraton Hotel, Sydney, (*left*); Jimmy Nicol is still deputizing for Ringo. In Adelaide (*below*) a serious George goes it alone and (*right below*) Ringo has recovered enough to join the other three boys for yet another press interview, but (*above*) the strain of touring is telling on Paul.

Above When the boys returned from their Far East tour at the beginning of July, only 200 fans turned up to greet them at London Airport – was this the beginning of the end?

Right Ringo celebrates his 24th birthday six days later with a carefully posed shot (note the hand on the floor).

Above Rehearsing their flying scene in mid-song for the charity show 'Night of 100 Stars' at the London Palladium Theater on July 23rd, 1964.

Left Sir Laurence Olivier joins the boys at their Palladium rehearsal.

Right Edwardian blazers and boaters for the Beatles at the Palladium.

Left On tour in the USA, August 1964, the Beatles play to an immense but orderly audience in Las Vegas. The tour lasted 32 days and was the longest, biggest and most exhausting of their career. They visited 24 cities in the US and Canada and gave a total of 30 performances plus one charity show (*below* and *right*).

Another day, another city, another show. Records were broken everywhere in the US but the Beatles were becoming trapped in the web of their own success; they could not move from their hotel without being mobbed and sat in their hotel bedrooms smoking, playing cards and their guitars, waiting for the next performance, the next move. One businessman from Kansas City offered first $100,000 and then, when that was turned down, $150,000 for the group to fit in an unscheduled stop in Kansas City. It was the highest fee ever offered to any artist in the US and Brian could not resist the prestige value – so they played another concert. The pillowslips on which they slept in Kansas City were sold to two businessmen, who cut them into one-inch squares and sold them for a dollar each.

Above Paul at the mike; however draining their schedule, the Beatles still get a buzz from performing.

Right above and below Rehearsing yet another show (*above*), surrounded by arc lights and scaffolding, while (*below*) the finished product is smooth and seamless.

Right One adoring young American fan's dreams come true. She is no doubt still telling her children that she was once cuddled by Paul McCartney.

Above Uniformed police surround the boys at their Las Vegas concert. The US police were more accustomed than their British counterparts to dealing with overwrought fans, from the wild days of the young Elvis Presley.

Right Focus on John.

Right Still smiling their best Beatle smiles, the four pose for photographs and sign autographs in Miami at their first of many press receptions.

THE BEATLES
IN AMERICA

THEIR OWN EXCLUSIVE STORY AND PICTURES

Right The fanzines of course had a field day following every step of their heroes' progress across the American continent.

Far left The only place to relax is the hotel bedroom on their US tour; (*above*) sunbathing is somewhat limited on a hotel balcony; (*below*) and what can you catch when you fish from a window?

Above Playing the one-armed bandits in Vegas – but Paul seems to be having a spot of bother.

Above Playing the Hollywood Bowl, another record-breaking concert.

Left A battery of mikes and an advance list of questions at yet another US press conference.

Right Cassius Clay, as he then was, does his 'I am the greatest' act over the prostrate Beatles; note the matching shoes.

Left A rare moment of relaxation in a swimming pool is still dogged by the inevitable photographers.

Above and right Accompanying the never-ending shows of summer and autumn 1964 came a host of new releases. Between the beginning of July and the end of August five singles were launched in the US to take advantage of the tour.

On tour in the US, the Beatles adopt cowboy gear; Ringo looks quite the expert saddling up his horse, and George seems thoroughly at home with the western-style mount.

Above Answering questions at a press reception in Miami, toward the end of their gruelling US tour. Their visit was hailed as one of the greatest Anglo-American diplomatic successes of the century. Their appeal to the ordinary American placed Britain in the unaccustomed limelight and Prime Minister Sir Alec Douglas-Home, who visited the US while the Beatles were there, referred to them as 'my secret weapon'.

Left Paul in the spotlight. At this stage the songwriting team of Lennon and McCartney was in full swing. The soundtrack of *A Hard Day's Night*, released in England in June and the US in July, featured twelve Lennon/McCartney numbers.

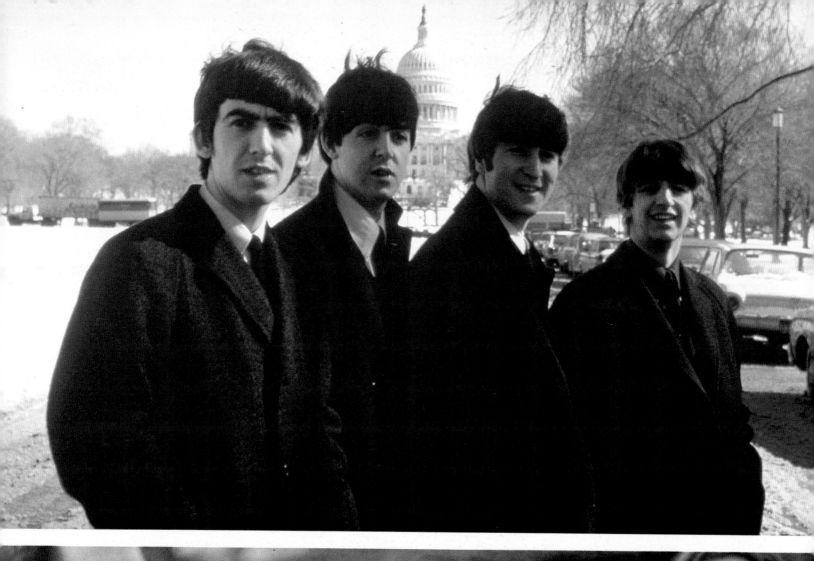

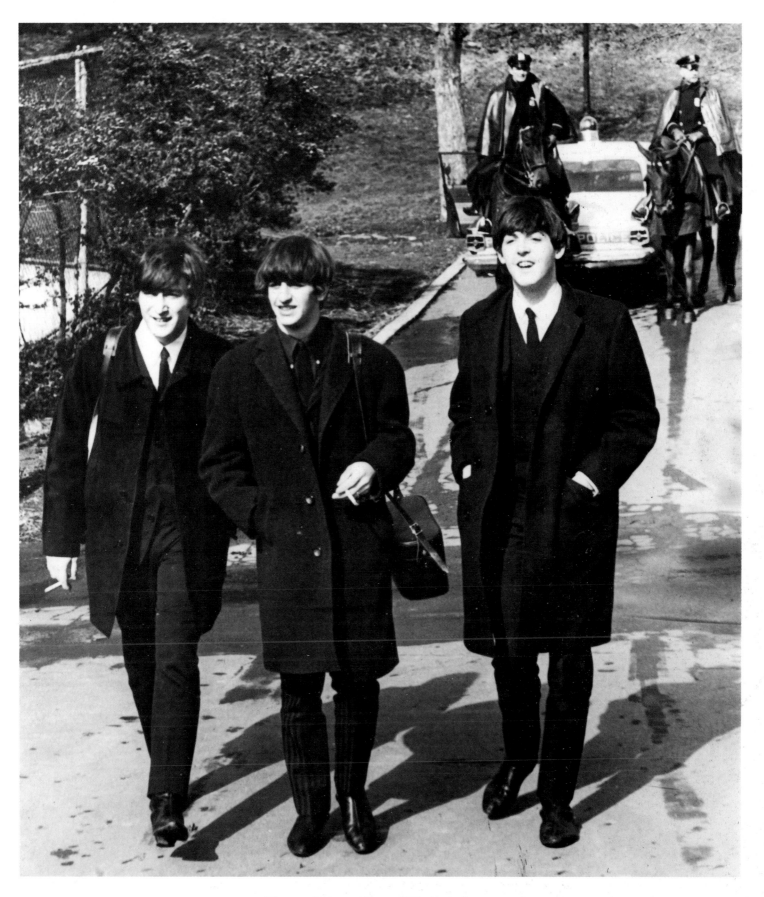

The cool atmosphere of their earlier
US trip in February 1964 belies the
hectic pace. The boys pose in the
snow in front of the Capitol,
Washington (*top left*); George yawns
hugely while Brian Epstein cultivates
anonymity in the background (*below
left*); and in New York (*above*) John,
Ringo and Paul manage a few
minutes' peace in Central Park.

In February 1965 Ringo married longtime girlfriend Maureen Cox in the London registry office of Caxton Hall. They had met in 1962 in Liverpool, where Maureen was a Cavern regular, and began to go out together almost at once. Like all Beatle wives and girlfriends, Maureen found she had to keep a low profile for her own safety; once her face was savagely scratched by an angry girl fan.

Right In the garden of the bungalow they borrowed for their honeymoon.

Below Brian Epstein, always watchful in the background, acted as Ringo's best man.

Far right A photocall the day after the wedding; Ringo is 26, Maureen 18.

Above The Beatles go public. In
February 1965 the firm Northern
Songs Ltd was launched to market
Lennon/McCartney songs, and was
instantly over-subscribed. Managing
Director Dick James reads the
Financial Times report, while (*right*)
staff struggle to cope with the share
applications.

Above right More gold and silver
discs and a Japanese doll each.

Left and above A winter photo
session for the Beatles in February
1965, just a few days before they flew
to the Bahamas to film their new film
Help!, at that time still called *Eight
Arms to Hold You.* The Triumph
Herald convertible, an English classic,
is quite a contrast to the American
convertible they were photographed
with just a year earlier.

Above and top right On the road
again, spring 1965. This time
Maureen Starr and Cynthia Lennon
go too.

Below right and far right The
seemingly unstoppable team of
Lennon and McCartney. Paul's ballad
'Yesterday' is about to hit the charts.

Left above and *below* The Beatles are
greeted with delight in Munich on
their 1965 European tour.

Top and *above* But the reality is very
different. Brian and Ringo wait for yet
another performance to begin (*top*),
and (*above*) the exhausted
entertainers relax wherever they can.

Above An informal shot of the famous
four in rehearsal gear at the studio,
recording the soundtrack for *Help!*

Right In April 1965 the Beatles
performed (*above*) and received
awards (*below*) at the *New Musical
Express* Poll Winners' concert at
Wembley, London.

NEW MUSICAL EXPRESS
POLL WINNERS CONCERT

NEW

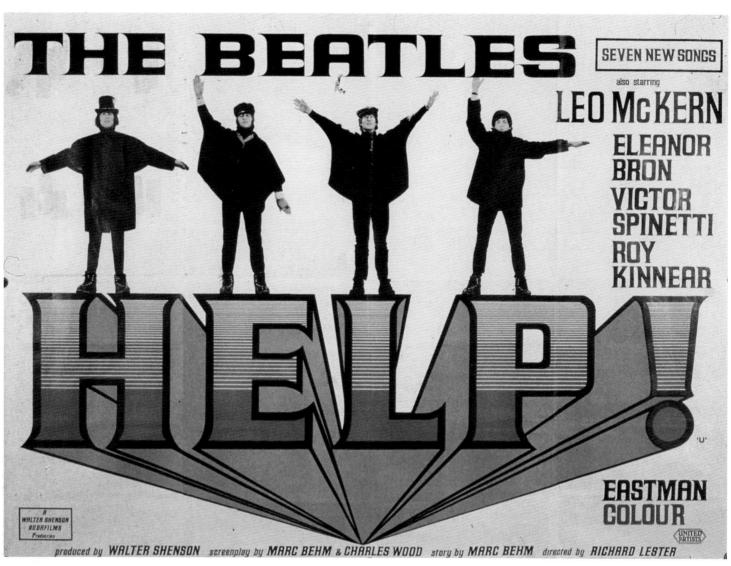

Left above Poster advertising the launch of the Beatles' second film *Help!*, released in July 1965.

Left below Dinner jackets for the Beatles and satin and fur for the two Beatle wives as they arrive for the West End premiere of *Help!* amid the usual scenes of tumult.

Right above and below The premiere was attended by Princess Margaret and her husband Lord Snowdon. The reviews were, of course, ecstatic, hailing the foursome as 'modern Marx brothers'.

Left A moody Paul strikes a James Dean attitude complete with motorbike.

This page Filming for *Help!*, the Beatles's second movie, quite as zany as *A Hard Day's Night*, moved from London to Salisbury Plain, then to Austria and the Bahamas – exotic locations were now well within the budget. But filming, even your own film, can be tedious (*above*), while exotic locations can prove confusing (*below*); Ringo and Paul puzzle over a travel guide to Nassau and the Bahamas.

The plot of *Help!* concerned the efforts of a Hindu murder sect to recover a ring which had become stuck on Ringo's finger, although like their previous film *A Hard Day's Night*, it was as much musical travelogue and Pop Art comic strip as straight film. Here the action moves to the ski slopes of Austria, an excuse for some glorious scenic photography and the usual clowning.

This page and overleaf Help! was again, like *A Hard Day's Night*, directed by Richard Lester and again the Beatles played themselves, but this time leading the kind of fantasy life that their fans expected.

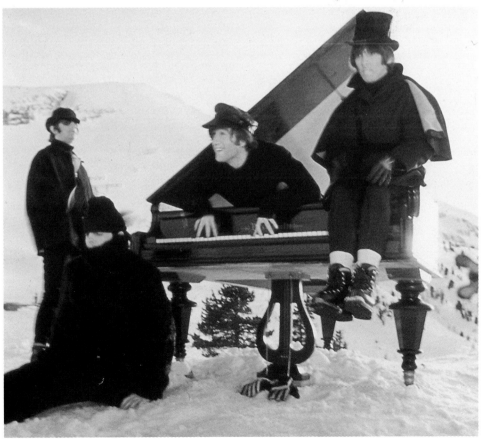

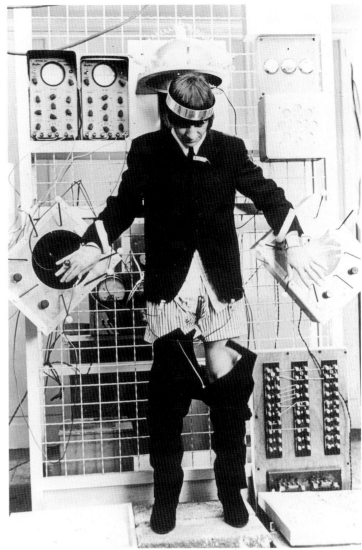

In their efforts to escape the bloodthirsty cult members who are determined to separate Ringo forcefully from the outrageous ring stuck on his finger, which just happens to be their sacred symbol, the Beatles adopt every possible kind of disguise. The promotional material ran: 'Why are the high priests of the terrible goddess of Kali interested in the Beatles? Why is Ringo being pursued to the ends of the earth by a gang of Eastern thugs? . . . Will John live to sleep in his pit again? . . . And Ringo – will he ever play the drums again?'

138

From snow to sunshine, the action of *Help!* moves from the snow-clad slopes of the Tyrol in southern Austria to the sun-drenched Caribbean islands.

Above and right The last week of filming for *Help!* took place at the beginning of May on Salisbury Plain, where the British army regularly exercise.

Above The cast of *Help!* included character actors such as Eleanor Bron, star of the satirical television show *That Was The Week That Was*. Here she is seen perched on a British army tank with our four heroes.

Below Ringo raves to an audience of one Centurion tank.

Above and *right* Unlike *A Hard Day's Night*, *Help!* was made entirely in color. The four were praised for their 'Chaplinesque' performances but in reality were simply being themselves.

Left Even in the colorful laid-back Bahamas George remains his private self.

Left above and below In summer 1965 the touring began again, to France, Italy, Spain and finally the US. On August 23rd the Beatles and Brian Epstein flew in by helicopter to Shea Stadium, the New York Mets' baseball ground, where a capacity audience of 55,000 awaited them. Even for the blasé Beatles this was triumph indeed.

Right Back home to family affairs – in the middle of September Maureen Starr gave birth to a son, Zak.

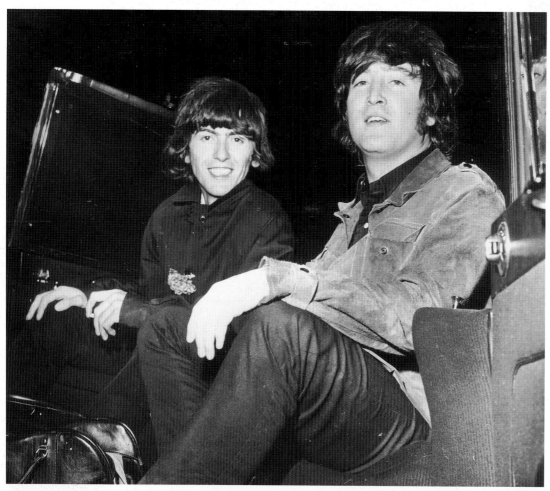

Left and below Another day, another airport. The Beatles return to London from their summer tour. The years 1965 and 1966 were dominated by touring; they averaged three long tours a year, one British, one American and one taking in a number of different countries. As Ringo said 'There were good nights and bad nights on tour. But they were really all the same.'

Right Ringo in summer 1965, with hair worn even longer than usual for the filming of *Help!*

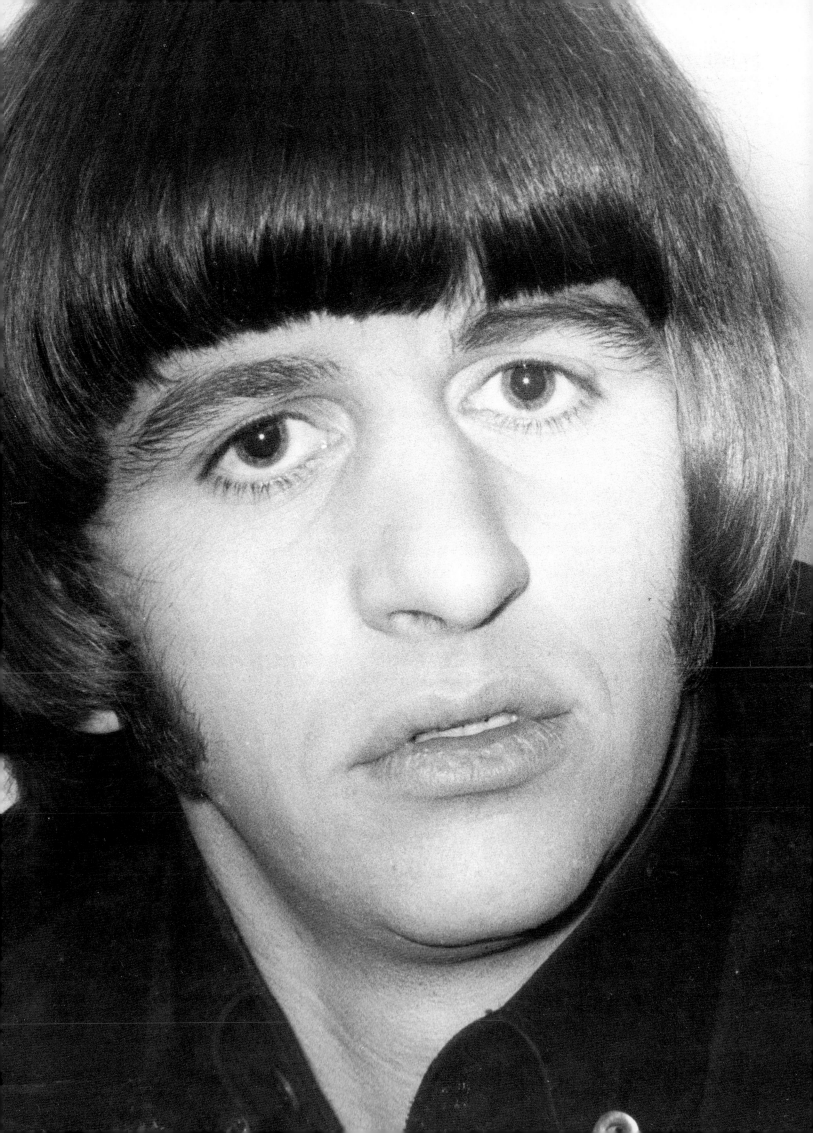

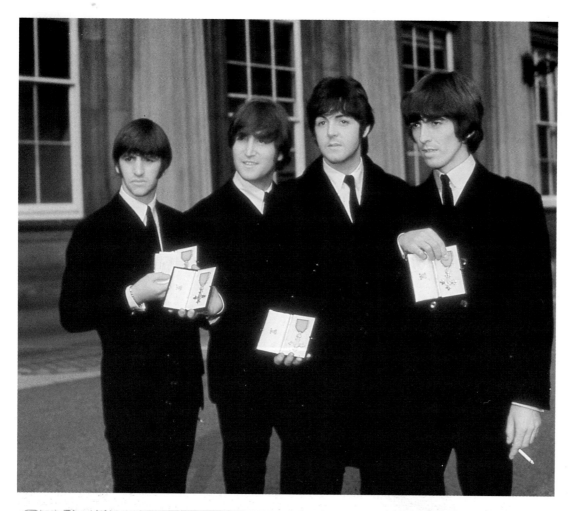

In June 1965 as part of the Queen's Birthday Honors, the Beatles were awarded the MBE (Member of the Most Excellent Order of the British Empire), an astute political move on the part of Britain's new Prime Minister, Harold Wilson, whose Labour Party had won the General Election of October 1964 after 13 years of Conservative rule.

Left above The Beatles outside Buckingham Palace after being presented by Queen Elizabeth with their MBEs.

Left below The crowd breaks through the police cordon and surges after the Beatles' car as it drives through the gates of the Palace before the ceremony; seconds later the police had to close the gates.

Right Afterwards the Beatles gave a press conference at the Saville Theater. 'I think it's marvelous', said Paul, 'What does that make my Dad?'

Left It was a typically cold and foggy
October day when the Beatles went
to the Palace to receive their awards.
They later admitted that they had
smoked cannabis in the palace toilets.

Above Some fan has managed to
catch the attention of all four as they
pass through yet another airport.

Large expensive houses are one of the perks of stardom. *Left above* Paul's house in St John's Wood, London, which he bought in 1965, undergoing extensive refurbishment before he moved in. *Left below* Ringo acquired this palatial establishment on the St George's Hill estate, Weybridge, part of the so-called stockbroker belt in pleasant rolling country south of London.

Above Earnest discussion during
recording of the Beatles' Christmas
television spectacular, 1965. Screened
on December 17, this consisted
wholly of Lennon/McCartney music
and lyrics, performed by a host of
famous artists. Paul opened the show
with his autumn hit 'Yesterday'.

PART 3
BRANCHING OUT
1966-69

In 1966 Brian Epstein wanted to schedule the Beatles' lives much as he had the previous two years; an album, followed by a movie, followed by a North American tour. But it didn't work out like that, and the Beatles never again functioned as the tight unit they were in the early 1960s. In April, however, they began work on the pioneering album 'Revolver', released in August, a 'concept' work featuring a remarkably eclectic group of songs arranged to form an integrated whole. On August 29 they gave what proved to be their last formal concert before a paying audience, in San Francisco. They then went their separate ways, John to make *How I Won the War*, George to India with wife Patti to study *sitar* with Ravi Shankar, Paul to write a film score – and Ringo to holiday.

But the story was by no means over; 1967 was the Beatles' most creative year yet. It began with the double A-sided single featuring 'Penny Lane' and 'Strawberry Fields' and reflecting the same vibrant and complex musicality that characterized 'Revolver'. Next came perhaps the best known album of them all, 'Sergeant Pepper's Lonely Hearts Club Band'. But 1967 also saw the death of Brian Epstein while the Beatles were in Wales meeting the Maharishi Mahesh Yogi; this proved the first step in the gradual unravelling of the huge commerical empire spawned by the Beatles' success. At first, however, all continued to go well. The crowning achievement of 1968 for Apple Corps was the album called 'The Beatles' but invariably known simply as the 'White Album'.

On January 21 1966 George married Patti Boyd, whom he had first met on the set of *A Hard Day's Night* at Twickenham sudios, south west London, in spring 1964.

Left Brian Epstein as best man congratulates the newly married George after the registry office ceremony.

Above The reception was held at George's home in Esher; this photograph shows Patti and George with George's parents and Patti's mother (seated in front).

Right George signs the marriage certificate.

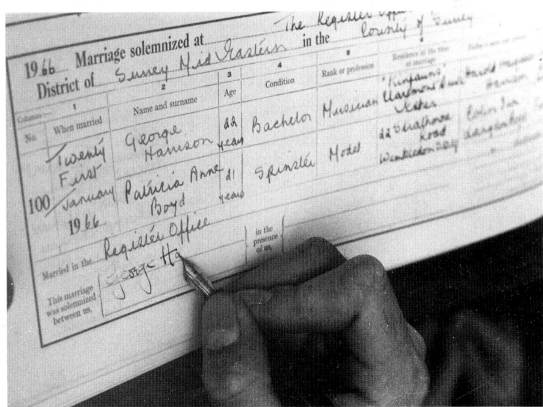

Above The Beatles recreate the session at which they recorded 'Paperback Writer' and 'Rain' for a color insert for US television's famous Ed Sullivan Show, on which they first triumphantly appeared in 1964.

Left George and Patti Harrison, after their wedding.

Right Paul escorts Jane Asher at the Plaza Theater, London, for the premiere of the film *Alfie*, starring Michael Caine. Paul had met Jane in 1963 and moved into her parents' home. They got engaged in late 1967 and Jane accompanied Paul to India, but the engagement ended soon after.

The Beatles planned to begin 1969 with a multi-media project, originally called 'Get Back', which saw the light of day only gradually and piecemeal. The increasing friction between John and Paul was highlighted by their marriages, within 10 days of each other, to two very different but equally influential women, Yoko Ono and Linda Eastman. 'Abbey Road', recorded summer 1969, was the last album the Beatles made together, and the final re-mix on August 20 was the last time that all four of them would ever be in the same studio at the same time.

Left June 1966: a live television appearance for the four boys before they set off on what is to prove their last international tour; their final live appearance was in the US on August 29.

Left below The 1966 tour included Hamburg as well as Munich and Essen in Germany, a rare chance to travel by train.

Left and above Pausing to wave at London Airport on their way to Germany; with 'Paperback Writer' topping the record charts in both Britain and the US, there is no doubt about the warmth of their reception.

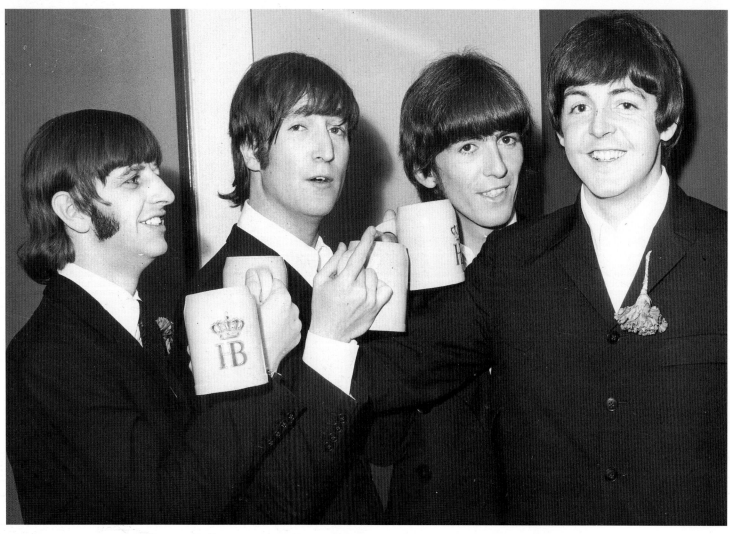

Above and right The Beatles star on *Top of the Pops*, BBC television's weekly pop show.

Left above August 1966 – the last tour of the US. Brian Epstein flew out a week earlier following an outbreak of 'Ban the Beatles' campaigns. John was reported to have claimed that the Beatles were more popular than Jesus.

Left below The only remaining bachelor Beatle, Paul celebrates his 24th birthday on June 18 1966.

By 1966 the Beatles were beginning to do their own individual things. John made another film with Richard Lester. This was *How I Won the War*, co-starring Michael Crawford, Roy Kinnear and Michael Hordern. Lester's usual mixture of black comedy and cinematic flourishes, *How I Won the War* concerned an earnest young man's tribulations during World War II. The film was made in Spain and John cut his hair for his non-singing role as Private Gripweed.

Far left above With co-stars Kinnear and Crawford.

Far left below Signing autographs for the cast.

This page Lennon and Kinnear in camouflage.

John in desert gear for *How I Won the War*. The film was less than rapturously received – one critic dismissed it as 'pretentious tomfoolery' – but Lennon's role was praised.

John's public saw a very different face from the Beatle Lennon in *How I Won the War*, but there was always time for some fooling and some photographs.

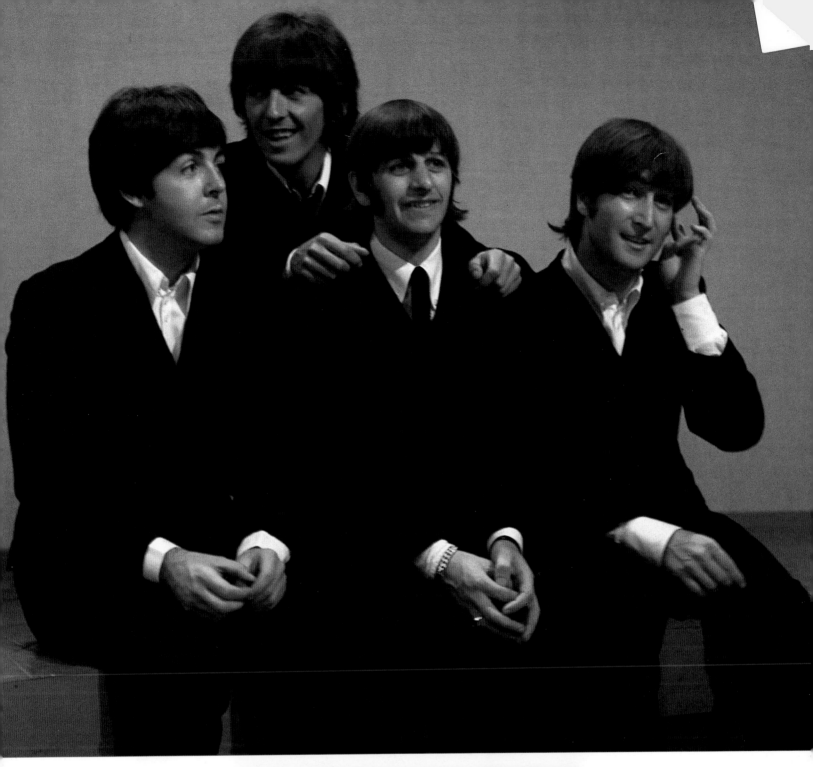

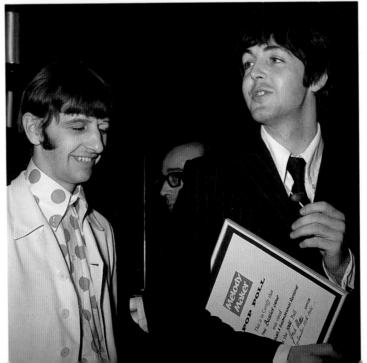

Left A serious John on set in his costume as Private Gripweed; the unfocused gaze is partly the effect of short sight – he is rarely seen without his characteristic granny glasses from now on.

Above The Beatles in 1966, the year that saw the release of their album 'Revolver'. This marked the start of a new development not just in the Beatles' music making but in the pop scene as a whole. It was presented, like no other previous pop album, as a continuous narrative and was a portent of things to come.

Left Paul and Ringo attend the Melody Maker awards in September, 1966; naturally the Beatles are award winners yet again.

John filming his role in a BBC
television Christmas spectacular with
the satirical comedy team of Peter
Cook and Dudley Moore.

Above John plays the part of a
lavatory commissionaire. The lavatory
is an exclusive one for members only;
Peter Cook (*right*) has to have his
credentials checked.

Left The Beatles in early 1967; John has kept the short haircut and granny glasses he donned for his role as Private Gripweed in *How I Won the War*. The era of love, peace and flower power is at hand and San Francisco groups such as Jefferson Airplane and the Grateful Dead are beginning to introduce British youth to the hippy happening.

Top The Beatles had a fallow period at the beginning of 1967; 'Penny Lane', for which the boys are here seen filming the promotional video, was recorded for the album 'Revolver' late in 1966, although only released as a single in the UK in February 1967.

Above Penny Lane; Paul's lyrics recreated exactly a part of Liverpool known to all four, including the barber who sold photographs.

Left Strawberry Fields was a Salvation Army children's home close to where John grew up, but his song was as much a hymn to the joys of LSD.

Filming for 'Penny Lane'; although a
double A-side, with 'Strawberry
Fields', the single was the first since
1962 not to reach the top of the
charts. Engelbert Humperdinck's
ballad 'Release Me' proved
immovable, but George Melly, jazz
musician and critic, described 'Penny
Lane' as pure poetry.

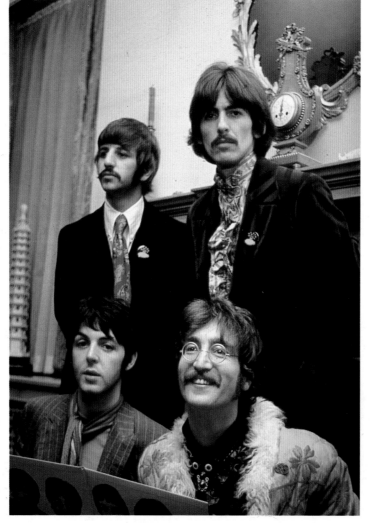

Above The 'Sergeant Pepper' album was launched in June 1967; the title song, 'Sergeant Pepper's Lonely Hearts Club Band', was inspired by the current fad for Victorian military uniforms and regalia. The idea of recording the whole album as though it were a real performance by the Sergeant Pepper band grew from that one song.

Left, right above and right below The Sergeant Pepper era soon developed its own momentum – the Beatles adopted Pepper gear, and the circus atmosphere was set by 'Being for the Benefit of Mr Kite', a Lennon composition suggested by an old theater bill. Another Lennon composition, 'Lucy in the Sky with Diamonds', owed more to LSD, with its images of tangerine trees and newspaper taxis. All four Beatles were well into LSD by now, hence in part the seamless presentation of the album.

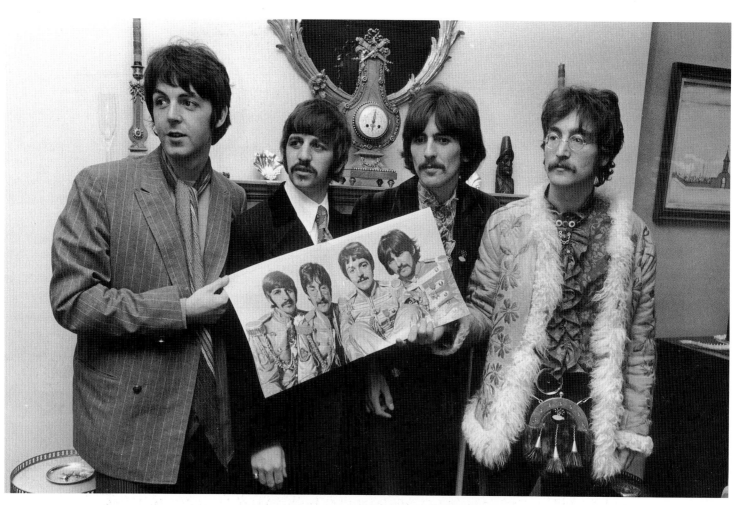

Left and above The recording
sessions for Sergeant Pepper were
conducted with a harmony soon to be
lost. Ringo and George both recorded
solos, Paul's main contribution was
'She's Leaving Home' and he and
John produced the first genuine
Lennon-McCartney collaboration for
some time with 'A Day in the Life'.

Left above Sergeant Pepper continues to rule.

Left below The young photographer seen chatting with Paul at the launch party for Sergeant Pepper is Linda Eastman, whom he marries two years later.

Above and right John Lennon's caravan, which he had decorated in suitably psychedelic colors in traditional gypsy style, is seen in the grounds of the Weybridge home he shared with Cynthia and son Julian.

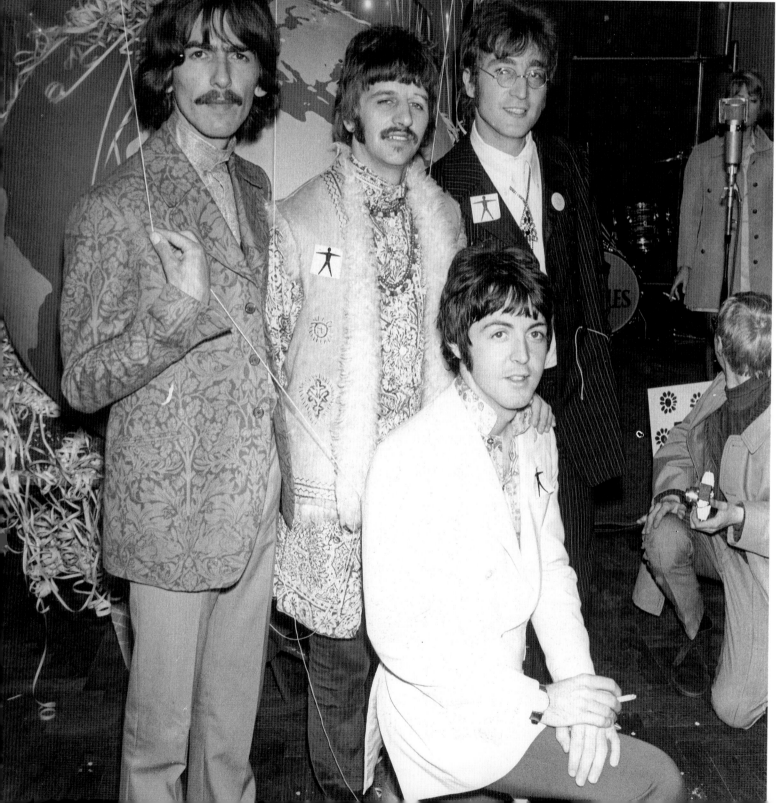

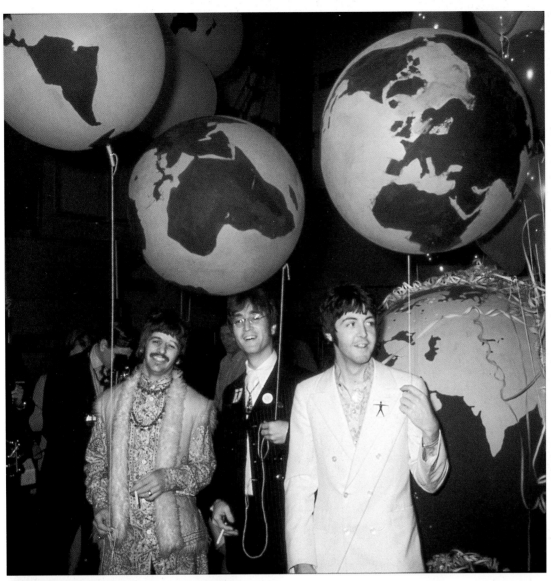

July 1967 saw the release of a new single, 'All You Need is Love', which followed Sergeant Pepper into chart history.

Far left above Rehearsing for the BBC contribution to 'Our World', a live global two-hour programme carried on four communications satellites on June 25.

Far left below At EMI's recording studios in Abbey Road, London, for the launch of 'All You Need is Love'.

Left and below left The Beatles with 'Our world' balloons.

Below right 'The Beatles are sitting at the next table!' – a break in the recording of 'All You Need is Love'.

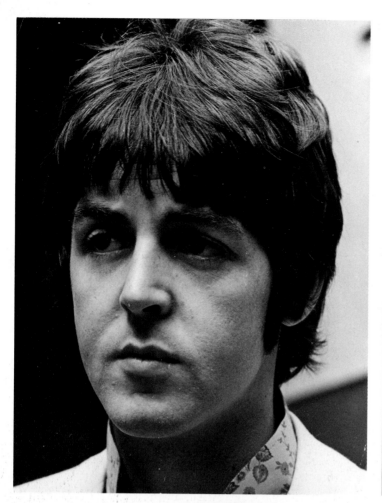

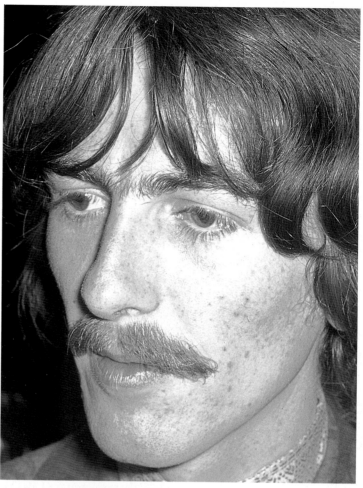

The boys in close-up during the 'All You Need is Love' summer: Paul (*above left*); George (*above right*); John, Ringo and George together in their billboards (*left*); Ringo (*below*); and John (*right*).

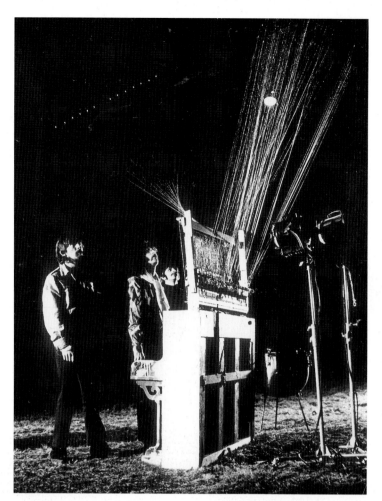

Right and below In September 1967 the boys began making their own film, which finally saw the light of day as the *Magical Mystery Tour*. They not only acted but directed and controled the extras. At a private hotel pool (*below*) John directs a number of chilly local girls in their bikinis.

Right Paul and Jane Asher returning to London after hearing of Brian Epstein's death in late August. The Beatles had met Maharishi Mahesh Yogi four days earlier and been enticed by his promises of inner peace and sublime consciousness to travel to Bangor, north Wales, for the August Bank Holiday weekend to attend a course for the Spiritually Regenerated. Together with Mick Jagger, lead singer with the Rolling Stones, they traveled to Bangor in the Maharishi's special train, the first journey they had ever made without Brian. Brian was found dead in bed on the Sunday morning by his housekeeper; the inquest verdict was an accidental drug overdose, although many other stories were told.

With the release of their new single 'Hello Goodbye' in November 1967 the Beatles also made a series of television films singing the song. The dancing girls (*above left*) are from a sequence for American release where the boys are wearing their Sergeant Pepper costumes. The more up-to-date Beatles look is shown right, where Paul and John do their 'Hello Goodbye' routine.

The Beatles were unusual on the pop scene for their long term relationships with girlfriends. Paul (*left*) was, for a long time linked with Jane Asher; they are seen here attending the opening night of the film *How I Won the War* on October 19 1969. Ringo (*right*) married Maureen Cox, while George and Patti Boyd (*below*) pose for the camera with John and Cynthia.

Crowds gather outside the Apple
shop in London's West End. The
corporation would eventually grow to
include the Beatles' musical, film and
publishing interests. The shop itself
opened at 94 Baker Street on
December 7 1967.

Above and left Two views of the Apple boutique, showing the *Mystical Goddess* mural and a crowd of bemused shoppers.

Below Paul takes a break from the filming of *Magical Mystery Tour*. The idea for the film was allegedly dreamt up by Paul during a return flight from the States.

These pages Magical Mystery Tour was conceived as a comedy about a group of circus acts and assorted hangers-on who tour the countryside in a bus and become involved in a series of misadventures. The outdoor scenes were shot in Cornwall during three days in September 1967; the interiors were filmed in several locations, including a former air base.

Below Paul with his Old English Sheepdog Martha pictured at the end of 1967, shortly after the showing of *Magical Mystery Tour* on television.

Right above and below In early 1968 the Beatles traveled to India to attend the Maharishi Mahesh Yogi's meditation center at Rishikesh. Disillusionment soon set in, however, and they cut short their stay. The band did manage to get some much-needed rest at the retreat and were also able to pen material for their next album.

Left and above The Beatles attending
the Maharishi's meditation center.
The trip turned into something of a
media exercise with innumerable
photographic calls. Ringo, perhaps
summing up the group's general
disappointment, described the retreat
as being like summer camp with
overspiced food.

Above The poster advertising the film *Yellow Submarine* in 1968.

Right John, Paul and Yoko Ono attend the premiere of *Yellow Submarine* at London's Pavilion Theatre on July 17.

Right above and below The Beatles publicize their film *Yellow Submarine*. The band are whisked off to 'Pepperland' where they battle against the 'Blue Meanies.'

Left, below and right The premiere of *Yellow Submarine* had everything: Blue Meanies, commissionaires on stilts, surging crowds, police cordons – and, of course, the Beatles. The boutique behind the yellow submarine (*below*) was part of the same craze for old-style military uniforms that inspired Sergeant Pepper.

Above The four Beatles – from left, John, George, Paul (looking more than usually cherubic) and Ringo – in the animated forms in which they appear in *Yellow Submarine*.

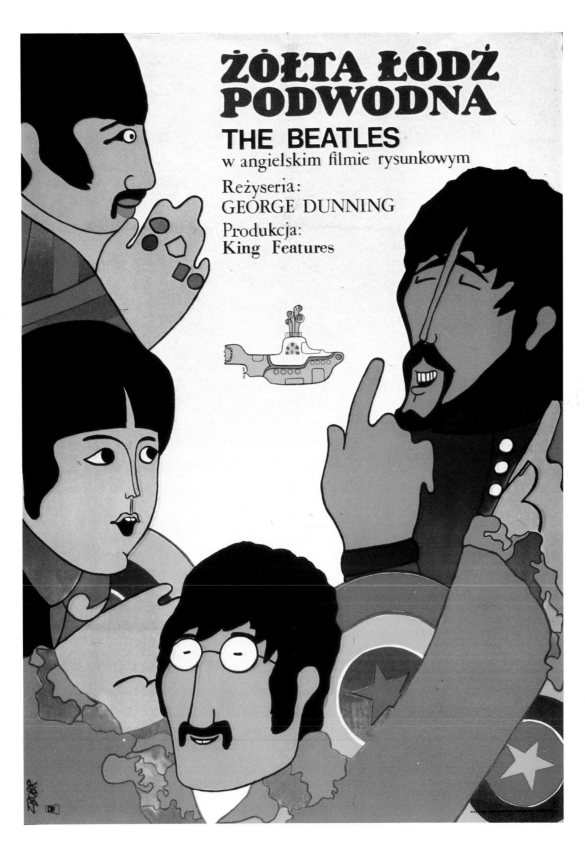

ŻÓŁTA ŁÓDŹ PODWODNA

THE BEATLES
w angielskim filmie rysunkowym

Reżyseria:
GEORGE DUNNING
Produkcja:
King Features

Yellow Submarine, though poorly reviewed at the time and denied a general release, has since achieved cult status. Written by Erich Segal, later a bestselling romantic novelist and author of *Love Story* (also memorably filmed), it translated Beatle lyrics into a genuinely original fantasy.

Left and below The premiere of *Yellow Submarine* was the usual scrum of photo calls and fans.

Right George and Patti Harrison arrive for the premiere of *Yellow Submarine*, bringing traffic to a standstill around Piccadilly Circus.

Left, below and right *Yellow Submarine* spawned a mass of souvenirs and imitations; the Beatles as little cartoon characters, with big eyes, buttons and neckties, became as well known and popular as the originals.

Left above and below From books to party coasters, *Yellow Submarine* produced the lot.

Above Ringo, George and Paul in relaxed and chatty mood at a press conference after the press preview of the film.

Left above The Apple boutique in July 1968; the *Mystical Goddess* mural has been covered in whitewash.

Left below In Summer 1968 the Beatles were occupied with the newly created Apple Corps to the exclusion of all else, even music-making. Here they launch a new group, Grapefruit, with the help of (from left standing) Brian Jones of the Rolling Stones, Donovan, and Cavern regular Cilla Black.

Above and right John and Paul spread the apple word at London Airport.

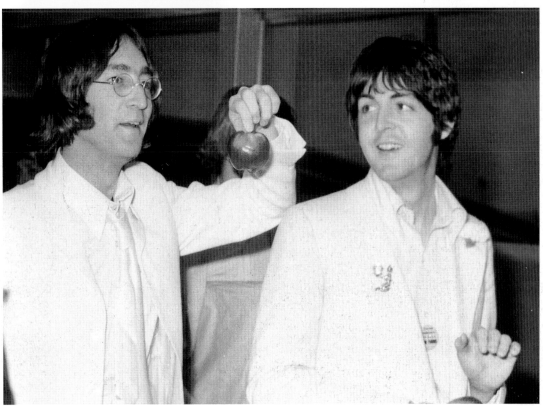

Ringo has a cameo role in *Candy*, based on the novel by Terry Southern. Co-stars include Sugar Ray Robinson as the barman (*below*) but the film was panned by the critics.

Left above One of the Apple record label's discoveries was the 18-year-old singer Mary Hopkin, seen here recording her hit 'Those Were the Days' with Paul McCartney, arranger Richard Newson and the Aida Foster Children's Choir.

Left below Despite the occasional venture into film, Ringo was more content than the others to stay quietly at home in his mock Tudor mansion in Weybridge, Surrey, where he had his own fully equipped bar, complete with till and beer on tap.

Above Artist John Bratby working on his portrait of Paul for display in the Royal Academy's Summer Exhibition.

Right The Fab Four in 1968, having abandoned the philosophy and flowers of the Maharishi, became whizzkid corporate executives, flying to New York to launch Apple Corps in the most crucial of its potential markets and to explain its revolutionary philanthropic motivation. Paul announced an Apple Foundation for the Arts, to help struggling artists achieve commercial success, and he and John enjoyed the novelty of more or less regular office hours, a desk and secretaries. While the Apple boutique slipped into chaos, and finally liquidated itself on July 31 by simply giving away its entire stock, Apple Records launched its first four singles, including Mary Hopkin's 'Those Were the Days' and the Beatles' own seven-minute long ballad 'Hey Jude'.

Above and right In October 1968 John and Yoko Ono, by now his regular companion, were arrested by Drug Squad officers and charged with possession of cannabis; John pleaded guilty at Marylebone magistrates' court and was fined £150. A month later Cynthia Lennon was granted a divorce on the grounds of John's adultery with Yoko.

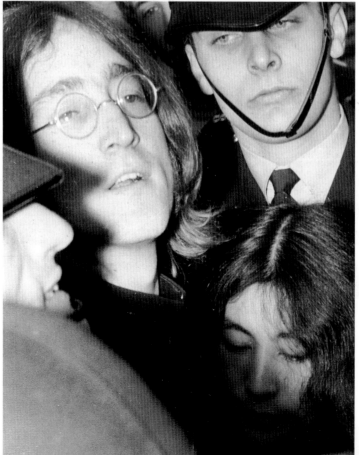

Right The impression given by this photo of four separate individuals rather than a group is an accurate picture of the Beatles in 1968. Recording sessions at the Abbey Road studios for what was to become known as the 'White Album' (released in November 1968) were made awkward by the constant presence of Yoko, and by the increasingly clear disparity in John and Paul's musical tastes. George's contribution was stronger than ever before; his final tally of four out of the 30 tracks was the highest John and Paul had ever allowed him.

Left John with Yoko and his son (by Cynthia) Julian watching circus acts at Intertel Studios, Wembley, north London. The Beatles were to be guest stars in a television spectacular tentatively called 'The Rolling Stones Rock 'n' Roll Circus Show' but never aired.

Above Pop notables watching a trapeze act include Bill Wyman, Charlie Watts and Brian Jones of the Rolling Stones, Keith Moon of The Who and Eric Clapton.

Right John performs with Clapton and Keith Richards of the Stones, and Mitch Mitchell on drums.

Above, right and far right
In March 1969 Paul married
Linda Eastman, whom he
had met two years
previously when she
photographed him in New
York. She and her six-year-
old daughter Heather had
moved into Paul's St John's
Wood house in the summer
of 1968, much to the
despair of the fans who
kept permanent vigil
outside the home of the last
bachelor Beatle. Heather is
pictured in the wedding
shot (*right*).

Left As Apple's finances deteriorated during the summer of 1969, the Beatles as a group continued to drift further apart. Here Ringo, always the quiet one, enjoys the millionaire's paradise of France's Côte d'Azur.

Above, left and overleaf
Meanwhile in March John had married Yoko and conducted a press conference from their bed in a hotel in Amsterdam.

Above John and Yoko recreating their
week spent in bed in Amsterdam in
protest for world peace for Eamonn
Andrews and Thames Television's
Today programme.

Right John, Yoko and Yoko's
daughter Kyoko leave London to
stage another seven-day 'Bed-in-for-
peace' in the Bahamas.

Left John and Yoko in 1969; they had launched their first solo experimental album through Apple the previous year.

This page The vast Georgian mansion, Tittenhurst Park in Berkshire, which the Lennons bought in 1969. It came complete with picture gallery, Tudor-style tea pavilion, tennis court, heated swimming pool and 72 acres of land.

Left Paul and Linda McCartney

Far left John and Yoko Lennon in Amsterdam shortly after their wedding.

Below John and Yoko cruising the Aegean in late 1969; here they are pictured on board a yacht in the harbour at Spetsae.

John and Yoko continued their peace campaign throughout 1969, culminating in a charity pop concert 'Peace for Christmas' on behalf of UNICEF (the United Nations Children's Fund).

Above and left At the UNICEF concert two of the Beatles appeared together on the stage for the first time since they gave up touring three and a half years before; George joins the Plastic Ono band (*above*).

Right As part of his and Yoko's peace campaign, directed particularly against the Vietnam War, John returned the MBE he had been awarded in 1965. Here they both pose on the steps of the Apple building in London's Savile Row with one of their posters.

Presenting the most
irreverent, irrelevant father and son team
since the Frankensteins.

Commonwealth United Presents a Grand Film Starring

Peter Sellers & Ringo Starr in "The Magic Christian"

with Guest Stars RICHARD ATTENBOROUGH · LEONARD FREY · LAURENCE HARVEY
CHRISTOPHER LEE · SPIKE MILLIGAN · RAQUEL WELCH
Also starring WILFRID HYDE WHITE · ISABEL JEANS · CAROLINE BLAKISTON
Produced by DENIS O'DELL · Directed by JOSEPH McGRATH · Executive Producers HENRY T. WEINSTEIN & ANTHONY B. UNGER
Screenplay by TERRY SOUTHERN, JOSEPH McGRATH & PETER SELLERS   From the novel by TERRY SOUTHERN
Music by KEN THORNE · Colour by TECHNICOLOR® · Released by COMMONWEALTH UNITED ENTERTAINMENT (UK) LTD
The Original Sound Track Album available on Commonwealth United Records   "Come and Get It" by PAUL McCARTNEY

In 1969 Ringo ventured into
the world of film again,
making *The Magic
Christian* (released in 1970)
with a star-studded cast
including Peter Sellers.

Above The poster; Ringo
played Sellers' son.

Left Princess Margaret paid
a surprise visit to the set of
Magic Christian in March
1969; here she watches
with producer Denis O'Dell
as a French restaurant
scene is set, before
lunching with producer and
cast.

In *The Magic Christian* Ringo plays
the son of an eccentric millionaire,
Peter Sellers, who devotes his wealth
to undermining those who pursue
money or power. The screenplay was
again based on a novel by Terry
Southern, who also had a part in the
film. Other stars included Raquel
Welch (*below left*).

Left and above left A family scene;
Paul and Linda McCartney and
Heather visit Ringo on the set of *The
Magic Christian*.

Above right A still from the film.

Right Paul and Linda with Ringo on the set of *The Magic Christian* in March 1969. The relaxed atmosphere is rare; although the year began well for the Beatles with the momentum generated by the 'Yellow Submarine' album, released in the UK and US in mid-January, and the 'White Album' still high, relations between the individual Beatles deteriorated during rehearsals for a grandiose multimedia project which finally saw the light of day in 1970 as 'Let It Be'. The lack of management direction which had led to the closing of the Apple boutique the previous summer was becoming increasingly obvious. John wanted to hire American record company executive Allan Klein to sort out the mess of Apple's finances, Paul favored the New York law firm run by Linda Eastman's father and brother. In the end both were appointed, Klein as business manager, Eastman and Eastman as legal advisers; the rift that was to develop between them paralleled the developing feud between John and Paul. In the course of all the politicking, Brian Epstein's brother Clive, now owner of the NEMS holding company, sold NEMS to the Triumph Investment Trust.

Left above Richard Attenborough,
Peter Sellers and Ringo in *The Magic
Christian*.

Left below Ringo and Sellers with
their offbeat friends.

Above A devoted father and son.

an intimate bioscopic experience with
THE BEATLES

APPLE
An **abkco** managed company
presents

"Let it be"

Left The 'Let It Be' album, finally
released in May 1970, over a year
after the series of recording sessions.

Above From left, Ringo, Paul, George
(standing), Yoko and John in the
recording studio; Yoko's constant
presence had become an intense
irritant.

Above and right The *Let It Be* film
was released in the UK and US in
May 1970. Film critics condemned it
as lacking in direction or coherence,
but as a documentary on the life of a
recording artist it was considered
priceless.

Left above and below, right
The focus is on John during the making of the *Let It Be* film and album. He chronicled his multimedia life with Yoko in 'The Ballad of John and Yoko', which the Beatles recorded in April 1969 and which proved to be the last song recorded specifically for release as a single. He and Yoko had already issued their first documentary album, 'Two Virgins', at the end of 1968; in June 1969 they issued their first single, 'Give Peace a Chance', credited to the Plastic Ono Band.

Overleaf 'Let It Be' was originally recorded under the name 'Get Back'; the tracks were completed by the end of February, the 'Get Back' single was released in April, but the album was first postponed and then shelved as Apple's affairs began to unravel. It was overtaken by 'Abbey Road', released in September in England and October in the US and almost instantly hailed as a masterpiece.

Above A gloomy looking Ringo at one
of the 'Let It Be' recording sessions;
the Beatles had to buy back the rights
that NEMS had to their royalties.

Right As the Beatles drift toward
break-up, George is doing some of his
best work for the 'White Album' and
'Abbey Road'.

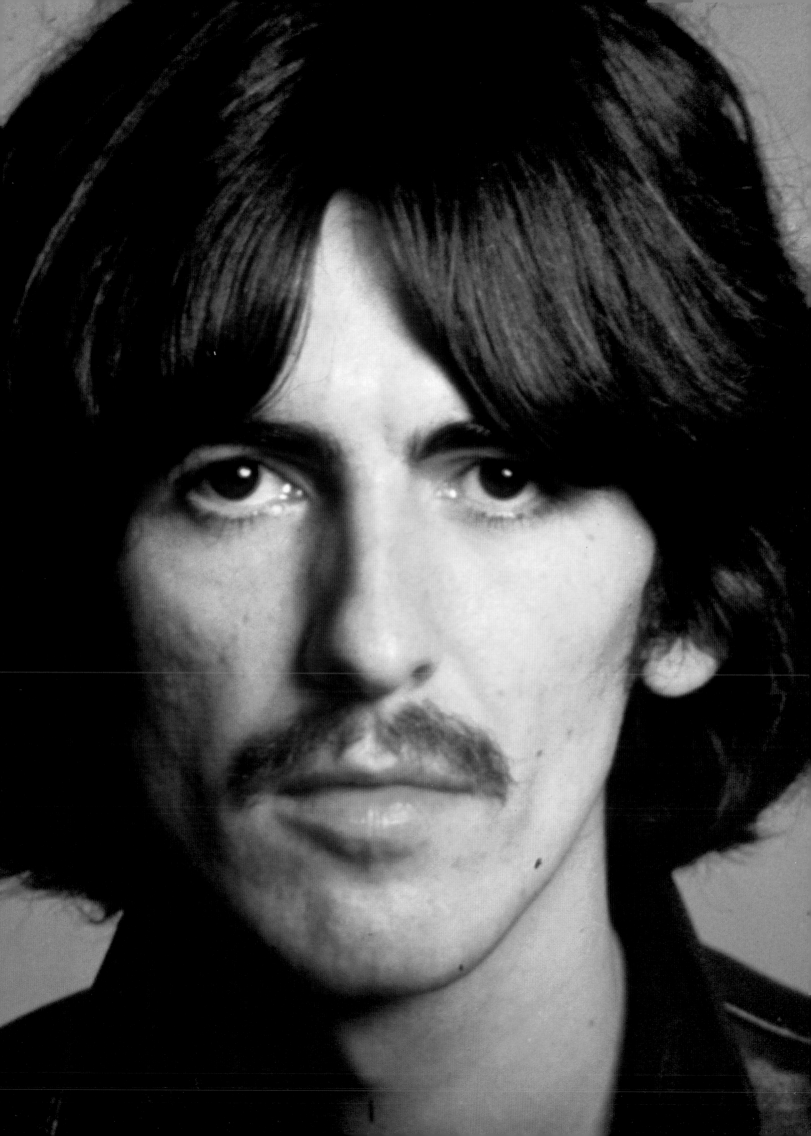

AFTERWARDS

1970 ON

It is hard to give a specific date for when the Beatles ceased to exist as an entity. 1970 began with rumors that they had already parted. In April Paul began to refer publicly to them in the past tense, and to all intents and purposes that was it. Although new Beatles albums were released that year, the only new material was on solo albums released by each individual Beatle. Ringo was the first, with 'Sentimental Journey' out in March. Paul's, called simply 'McCartney', was the first mainstream rock album to be produced by an individual Beatle and was seen by many as competition for the 'Get Back' tapes. These finally saw the light of day as the 'Let It Be' album, 'reproduced' by Phil Spector, and seemed an anticlimax after the yearly succession of milestone albums beginning with 'Rubber Soul' in 1966.

The biggest individual release of 1970 was George's 'All Things Must Pass', a three-record set on which he was backed by some of the best rock musicians available, including Eric Clapton and Duane Allman on guitar – and Ringo Starr on drums. For years Harrison the songwriter had been overshadowed by the towering success of the

Left One of the last pictures of the four Beatles together. By the time 'Abbey Road', the last album they made though not the last to be released ('Let It Be' finally appeared in spring 1970), hit the shops in autumn 1969 they had gone their separate ways. The formal end came on December 31, 1970, when Paul filed suit against the Beatles partnership in order to end his relationship with the group.

Right above and below, far right The Plastic Ono Band was the name John used for the many bands he recorded with in the 1970s but he, and occasionally Yoko, were its only permanent members. In December 1970 he released his first all-rock, non-experimental solo album, simply called the 'Plastic Ono Band', a deeply personal and introspective work.

Left John and Yoko in the snow of north Jutland, Denmark, while visiting Yoko's daughter Kyoko.

Below Paul's house in St John's Wood in leafy north London; the pints of milk suggest someone is in residence but Paul and Linda spent more time on his farm in Scotland.

Right above A newly shorn John hands his hair to Black Power leader Michael X so that it can be auctioned for peace; February 1970.

Right below The new look John and Yoko.

Lennon/McCartney partnership; this was his response and by far his best solo album.

As significant for John as 'All Things Must Pass' for George was his 'Imagine' album, released September 1971 and a striking a keynote for the rest of the decade. He and Yoko, both separately and together, recorded prolifically during the early 1970s, but the birth of their son Sean in 1975 led to a period of semi-seclusion until the release of their 'Double Fantasy' album on November 17 1980; a new beginning destined to be cut short by an assassin's bullet just three weeks later.

Ringo continued to make albums in the 1970s but also diversified into film and property. It was left to Paul to carve out a second career as a rock musician, with the formation of a new group, Wings, in 1971. His musical fantasy film *Give My Regards to Broad Street* came closest of all ex-Beatle films to reviving the idiosyncratic light-heartedness of *A Hard Day's Night* and *Help!* The soundtrack featured new versions of five songs he had recorded with the Beatles, as well as more recent songs and all-new material.

Above John's short hair and granny
glasses recall the look he adopted for
Private Gripweed in *How I Won the
War* (1966).

Left Ringo released his first solo album, 'Sentimental Journey', in March 1970, mainly featuring vintage standards that he had sung with his family as a child. He too played the peace game (*left above*) but also found time to attend Mick Jagger's wedding to Bianca Perez Moreno de Macias in St Tropez with his wife Maureen (*above right*).

Above and left George cements his link with Indian arts and music at the press reception to launch the first festival of Indian arts to be held in the UK, September 17, 1970; he is seen with seven leading Indian instrumentalists and singers. His three-record set 'All Things Must Pass', on which he was backed by some of the best musicians in the world, including Eric Clapton and Ringo on drums, was released at this time, confirming his songwriting talents.

Right Ringo launches into design; here he is seen in 1971 touring an exhibition of steel furniture designed by himself and Robin Cruikshank which was mounted in Liberty's, one of London's premier department stores.

Left The Beatles continued to perform
as individuals after the break-up of
the group. George with Eric Clapton
(*left above*) at the UNICEF
Bangladesh relief concert in August
1971; and John with Elton John in the
mid-1970s (*left below*).

Above Yoko as authoress at a book-
signing session.

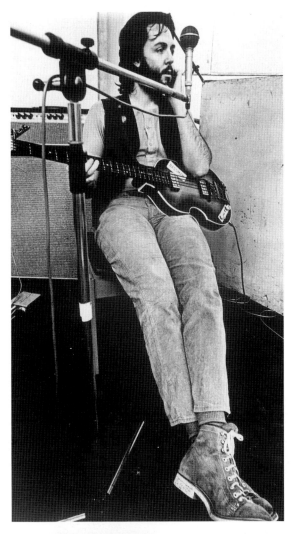

In the 1970s Paul embarked on a staggeringly successful second career. A solo album, 'McCartney', on which he played all the instruments, was followed by 'Ram' with Linda. In 1971 he formed a new group, Wings, and went back on the road.

John released his album 'Imagine' in
September 1971; its title track was in
many ways his most memorable post-
Beatle work. He and Yoko spent the
next few years in New York's
Greenwich Village, making albums
and avant-garde home movies. His
relationship with May Pang, a
Chinese-American woman whom the
Lennons had hired as a valet/
secretary, began to take him
increasingly to Los Angeles.

Ringo made a number of albums in the early 1970s, of which 'Ringo' (1973) was the most successful. He asked each of the other ex-Beatles to write a song for him, and at different times each of them joined him in the recording studio, although Lennon and McCartney never coincided. His acting career continued with a part in another rock film, *That'll Be the Day*, with pop star David Essex. The film begins in the 1950s, and here Ringo and Essex sport the right gear and sideburns.

That'll Be The Day tells the story of a young drifter (David Essex) who becomes a fairground worker and eventually walks out on his wife and family to become a pop star. It was greeted as a welcome return to British realism, with its dour but sympathetic viewpoint. As well as Ringo it starred Billy Fury, a fifties original.

Nat Cohen presents an Anglo EMI Film
Goodtimes Enterprises production

That'll Be The Day

starring

DAVID ESSEX
ROSEMARY LEACH
RINGO STARR

Guest stars
JAMES BOOTH **BILLY FURY**
KEITH MOON

EMI

Executive Producer ROY BAIRD
Directed by CLAUDE WHATHAM
Original story and screenplay by RAY CONNOLLY
Produced by DAVID PUTTNAM and SANFORD LIEBERSON

Technicolor *

Distributed by Anglo EMI Film Distributors Limited

273

Above After a wild couple of years in Los Angeles, during which he recorded two albums, 'Mind Games' (1973) and 'Walls and Bridges' (1974), John was reconciled with Yoko and in October 1975 their son Sean Ono Tara Lennon was born. Here John and Yoko are seen in rare evening rig with Andy Williams.

Left These four boys appeared as Sergeant Pepper era Beatles in a musical in 1979.

Right George in Amsterdam with the inevitable tourist clogs.

275

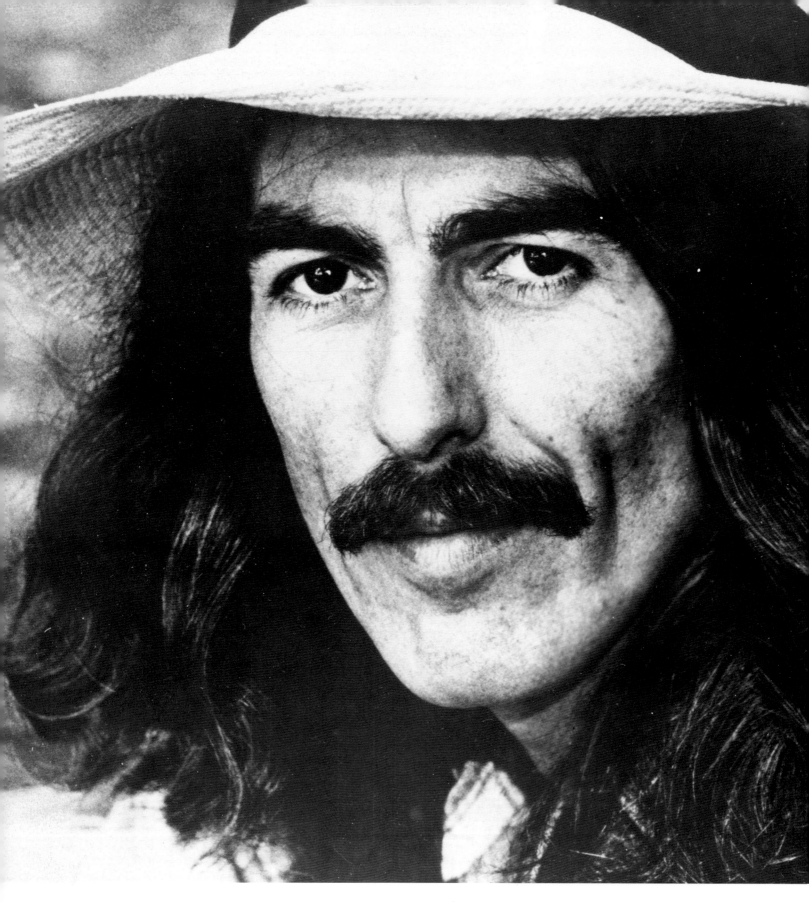

Previous page In the late 1970s John and Yoko concentrated on family life, which included frequent escapes to their Palm Beach estate from their New York apartment.

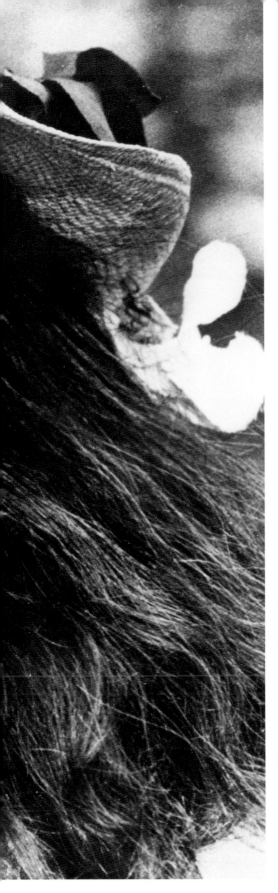

Left and above In 1975 George toured
North America, his first tour since the
last one with the Beatles nine years
before. The tour coincided with the
release of his album 'Extra Texture',
and in 1976 he started his own label,
Dark Horse, the title of his 1973
album. He released three albums
between 1979 and 1982, then retired
for five years, re-emerging in 1988
with 'Cloud Nine'.

Above and left Paul recorded nine albums with his new group Wings during the 1970s, making him much the most prolific ex-Beatle, and he also took on the occasional purely commercial project, such as the title song for the soundtrack of the 1973 James Bond movie *Live and Let Die*.

Right Ringo doing his own thing on Dutch television in 1976.

Faces of Paul; many critics felt that his work with Wings was weak and flaccid after the abrasiveness of the Lennon/McCartney combination, but his single 'Mull of Kintyre' has become the top-seller of all times, relegating 'She Loves You' to second place.

Left George in action in the late 1970s.

Below Ringo pursuing his acting career with new wife Barbara and some of the lovelies who starred in the various James Bond films.

Right Four ex-Beatles: clockwise from top left, Paul in the studio; John shortly before his death; a contemplative George, who has remained committed to Eastern mysticism; and Ringo in action at the mike.

Far left, above left and right
Ringo's recording career
declined in the late 1970s
and in 1979 he became
seriously ill with a
recurrence of the peritonitis
he suffered as a child.

Left Paul in 1980 with Yul
Brynner, star of *The King
and I*, who presented him
with an Ivor Novello
Award.

EXTRA EXTRA

NEW YORK POST

TODAY
Chance of showers, 45-50

TONIGHT
Rain, 35-40

TOMORROW
Partial clearing, 40-45
Details, Page 2

TV listings: P. 63

TUESDAY, DECEMBER 9, 1980 **25** CENTS + x AMERICA'S FASTEST-GROWING NEWSPAPER

METRO
TODAY'S RACING

700,000

JOHN LENNON SHOT DEAD

JOHN LENNON

The 40-year-old ex-Beatle was shot and killed late last night in front of his home on the Upper West Side.

Gunned down by 'screwball' outside home as wife Yoko watches in horror

DRAMATIC COVERAGE: PAGES 2, 3, 4, 5, 31, 32, 33

On December 9 1980 John Lennon
was shot dead outside his New York
apartment as he returned from a
recording session; the album that he
and Yoko were working on, their first
since the birth of Sean, was finally
released in 1984 as 'Milk and Honey'.

Top Thousands of mourning fans surround his New York apartment after the news of the killing of John Lennon.

Left Russian fans pay tribute to Lennon.

Above Julian Lennon with Yoko and Sean at the 1985 launch of a home video of Julian's first-ever concert tour.

Right Flowers accumulate outside John's apartment after the shooting.

In April 1981 Ringo married American
actress Barbara Bach. His marriage to
Maureen had ended in 1975 and he
met Barbara on the set of *Caveman*,
which he made the previous year,
playing the leader of a group of misfit
cavemen. Both George and Paul
attended the ceremony.

Left Paul at his farm near Rye, Sussex, shortly after he and Linda were arrested in Japan for carrying cannabis and deported after ten days in jail.

Right Ringo joins Linda and Paul backstage at a Wings concert. In 1979 the *Guinness Book of Records* presented him with a rhodium disc as the most successful composer of all time and the holder of the largest number of gold discs.

Left Julian and Sean Lennon are following in the family footsteps.

Far left Ringo dressed as a Mexican during a tourist trip to Copenhagen.

Above Ringo with his co-star Tony Anthony on the set of *Blindman*, a spaghetti western in which Ringo plays the villain who has stolen 50 women from a blind cowboy with a seeing-eye horse.

Left A gold disc for Ringo solo.

Above and right Paul's one venture into film was *Give My Regards to Broad Street* (1984), in which he starred with Tracey Ullmann. Paul funded the project, in which he played an international rock star who loses the priceless tapes of his new album and searches London for them. Essentially a platform for Paul's musical talents, the film also featured Ringo and his wife Barbara Bach.

Left This recent shot of Paul, taken in 1987, shows the smoothly tailored, immensely successful musician and businessman he has become.

Above George's hideaway in Maui, Hawaii.

Right George with new wife Olivia Arias. His marriage to Patti Boyd ended when Patti left him for Eric Clapton.

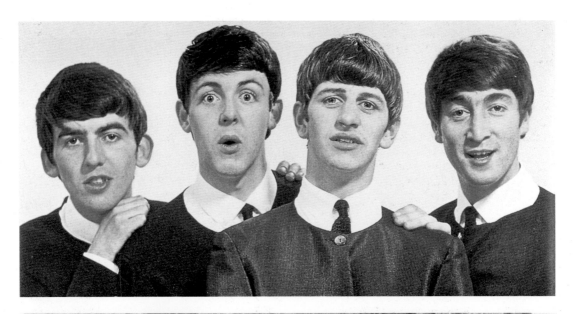

Top The early days: the Beatles at
the start of it all in 1963, in their
Beatle jackets and mop haircuts.

Above One of the last shots of all four
Beatles together; once the
relationship was formally dissolved
Lennon and McCartney never met
again.

INDEX

ACKNOWLEDGMENTS

American Graphic System: pages 10 (bottom), 41 (top left and bottom right), 45, 58 (top left and right), 66 (four), 74 (top), 78 (top), 79 (bottom left and right), 120, 121 (bottom left and right), 129 (bottom), 132 (top), 141 (top), 221 (bottom), 268, 269 (top left and right, bottom right), 276 (top right), 278, 279, 282 (all four), 283, 285 (top right), 286, 287 (top left), 290 (bottom right), 293, 295 (top), 297 (bottom), 298, 299 (both), 300.

British Film Institute: pages 10 (top left, center right), 11 (bottom left), 65 (top), 67 (both), 68 (bottom), 71 (both), 74 (bottom), 75 (bottom), 78 (bottom), 79 (top), 81 (top), 87 (bottom), 126 (top), 130 (both), 131 (both), 132 (both), 133 (both), 134, 136 (both), 137 (three), 138 (both), 139, 140 (both), 141 (bottom), 142 (top left), 143, 162 (both), 163 (both), 164 (three), 165, 166 (three), 167, 168, 195 (top, center, bottom right), 200 (top).

Hulton-Deutsch Collection: pages 2, 2/3, 4/5, 7 (top), 8 (all), 11 (bottom right), 13 (bottom), 26 (top), 28 (bottom), 29 (both), 30 (bottom), 31, 32 (both), 33 (both), 34, 35 (left), 36 (both), 37 (both), 38 (top left and right), 40, 42 (top), 43 (center), 44 (both), 46 (right and top left), 47 (top), 48 (both), 49 (three), 50 (both), 51, 52 (both), 56 (both), 57 (both), 59, 60, 61, 62 (both), 63 (both), 64, 65 (bottom), 69 (top), 72, 75 (top), 81 (bottom), 82 (both), 83 (both), 86 (top), 88, 89 (both), 91 (top), 92, 93, 94 (both), 96 (both), 98/9, 100 (top), 101 (both), 102 (top), 103, 104 (both), 105 (top), 106 (both), 109 (both), 111 (top), 113, 114 (both), 115, 116, 117 (both), 118 (both), 119, 121 (top), 122 (both), 123 (both), 125 (both), 126 (bottom), 127 (bottom), 128, 129 (top), 142 (bottom), 144 (both), 145 (top), 146 (both), 147, 148 (both), 149, 150 (both), 151, 153, 154, 155 (both), 156, 157 (both), 158 (both), 159 (both), 160 (both), 170, 171, 176 (top), 177 (both), 178 (both), 179, 180 (both), 181 (both), 182 (top), 183 (top and bottom left), 184 (bottom left), 186 (bottom), 187, 188 (both), 189 (both), 190 (bottom), 192, 193 (both), 194 (both), 195 (bottom left), 196 (top left and right), 197 (top), 198 (both), 200 (bottom), 202 (top), 203 (top), 207 (top), 209, 210 (both), 211 (both), 214 (both), 215, 218 (both), 220, 221 (top), 222 (top), 223, 224, 225 (both), 228, 229, 230, 231 (three), 233 (both), 234 (both), 235, 236 (bottom), 258 (both), 259 (both), 260, 261 (top right), 262 (both), 263, 264 (bottom), 265, 267 (top right), 274 (bottom), 285 (top right), 287 (top right and bottom), 289, 290 (top and bottom left), 291, 292 (both), 294, 296, 297 (top).

Pictorial Press Ltd: pages 1, 6 (both), 7 (bottom), 9 (both), 10 (top right), 11 (top and center), 12 (three), 13 (top), 14 (three), 15, 16, 17 (both), 18 (three), 19 (both), 20 (both), 21 (both), 22 (both), 23, 24 (both), 25, 26 (bottom left and right), 27 (three), 28 (top three), 30 (top three), 35 (three right), 38 (both), 39 (both), 41 (top right and bottom left), 42 (bottom), 43 (top and bottom), 46 (bottom left), 47 (bottom), 53 (both), 54, 55 (both), 58 (bottom), 68 (top), 69 (bottom), 70 (three), 73, 76, 77 (four), 80, 84, 85 (both), 86 (bottom), 87 (bottom), 90 (both), 91 (bottom), 95, 97, 100 (bottom), 102 (bottom), 105 (bottom), 108, 110 (both), 111 (bottom), 112 (both), 124, 127 (top), 142 (top right), 145 (bottom), 152 (both), 161 (both), 169 (both), 172, 173 (three), 174, 175 (both), 176 (bottom), 182 (bottom), 183 (bottom right), 184 (top left and right, bottom right), 185, 186 (top), 190 (top), 191, 196 (bottom), 197 (bottom), 199, 201 (both), 206 (both), 207 (left, bottom left and right), 209 (both), 216, 219, 222 (bottom), 226/7, 232, 238 (top), 239, 240, 241 (left), 242/3, 244 (bottom), 247, 255, 256, 257 (top and bottom left), 261 (top left), 264 (top), 266, 274 (top), 275, 276 (top left and bottom), 277, 280 (both), 281, 284 (both), 285 (bottom left and right), 288, 295 (bottom), 301 (both), 302 (both).

UPI/Bettmann Archive: page 107.

BLADEN COUNTY PUBLIC LIBRARY

T 59689

781.66
D
Delano
The Beatles album

C.1

6-92   2-1-94